"If we couldn't laugh, we would all go insane."

~Robert Frost

"Be kind, for everyone you meet is fighting a great battle."

~Author uncertain

"There is a thin line that separates laughter and pain, comedy and tragedy, humor and hurt."

~*Erma Bombeck*

"I really loathe *everything* about root beer."

~*Dan Pearce*

The All-Important
WELL-FED
Giant White Man

a memoir

DAN PEARCE

A Single Dad Laughing Book
Salt Lake City, Utah

DEDICATION & ACKNOWLEDGEMENTS

This book is dedicated to me, first and foremost. Yes, that's probably strange. I know. But you know what? I actually had to *learn* how to finally like myself enough to be willing to write much of what you'll read herein. Writing it was something I *had* to do for my own happiness, liberation, and understanding. And, I think that was truly badass of me to pull off, don't you?

I *also* dedicate this book whole-heartedly to my son. Noah. I know that no person will shape him, his view of the world, and life the way his own father will, and I hope that the stories and lessons found on these pages will one day give him a perspective and unique view of life that will help him have a truly authentic and content existence.

Finally, I dedicate this book to every person who contributed to making me who I am, and particularly those who have found their way into this memoir:

To Mom and Dad who had the toughest job of all, and whom I love deeply. My parents rock. Sorry for all the f-bombs. Kind of.

To Tomi Ann, my older sister, and Eric, my younger brother. I have 9 siblings, but these two were closest to me in age and had more effect on me than any others as we grew up. They are the best kind of humans. All you other siblings, don't get butt-hurt. I love your guts, too.

To my closest friends. Friends have always carried me through this life and my hardest moments. Good friends are the world to me. You know who you are.

To my child's mother who is dedicated to teaching our son goodness, and who was selfless enough to give me her blessing to share some intimate and private details of our relationship with all of you.

To all the women who have come and gone from my life. For the broken hearts I've given and received. For the failed romances and the many friends I have from them still. I have a permanent place in my heart reserved for so many of you. You also know who you are.

And for my readers. All of you. You have been so supportive over the years. I hope this book gives back to you something amazing as well. If not, let's just pretend someone else wrote it.

CONTENTS

The All-Important,
Well-Fed,
Giant White Man

INTRODUCTION
Escaping Death

When I was not yet three, Dad let go of my hand after our family had finished crossing a busy intersection, and turned his focus for the shortest moment to Mom and my other two young siblings. "Stay here," he told me.

To some this would be considered a lousy parenting moment. To me, after a lifetime to ponder it, and now that I'm a parent myself, I consider it... a lousy parenting moment.

He turned back around just in time to watch me sprint as fast as two-year-old legs can toddle, straight into heavy traffic.

A big, heavy, old-school Camaro was flying through the intersection and was *maybe* twenty feet away, going full speed straight at me when I entered the street.

I should have been dead less than one second later.

There was no way for the driver of the Camaro to even hit the brakes before he got to me, let alone bring his car to a stop in time.

The thought of the flashflood of dread which must have flooded both my parents in that moment makes my own fatherly stomach churn. I mean, before you can even think the thought, to know that you are about to witness your child's face splat against a car's bumper... I don't want to envision how that must have felt. Probably the way I felt when Michael Jordan jumped for a three pointer at the buzzer just before he took away my team's chance at the national title. Utah was almost cool there for a minute. And okay, Mom and Dad's moment was probably worse.

I didn't get hit by the car. As if some invisible force stepped in, the Camaro just stopped dead in its tracks. And stopped isn't even the right word. That would invite images of somehow slowing down, even if dramatically, and *then* stopping. No, it just went from full-speed to dead-still as if it had hit a wall of impenetrable air.

But, get this. There was *nothing* there to stop it. At least not anything that could be seen by the naked eye. And it happened just a foot or so before the fender made impact with my chubby little unsuspecting mug.

Dad and Mom always told the story and said it was as if angels had stood between me and the car. I think Mom definitely believes that to be the case. How else do you explain such a crazy phenomenon? God *obviously* wanted me alive. Not to brag or anything. I'm *obviously* a pretty fucking important person.

A few months later, I was alone in the living room while Mom prepared dinner, and I began playing behind the brown and yellow floral curtains. While standing bare-footed on a heating vent, I grabbed the frayed cord of a hanging lamp that was plugged in next to me, and I began gnawing on it as any intelligent three-year-old would.

I was immediately electrocuted.

Mom came out to check on her kids and saw my arm extending from beneath the curtain. "Get out of there, Danny!" she shouted at me. I didn't move. "Danny, come on, get out of the curtains!" she demanded again. Still I did not move.

She yanked the curtains back, ready to give me a thorough chewing and found my unconscious tiny gray body, clumped on the floor. My eyes were rolled back into my head. Panicked, she shook me. I showed no signs of life. In that moment, Mom probably felt she was holding her dead child.

I don't think I ever fully appreciated the weight of that until my own son, Noah, came into my life.

In a panicked frenzy, she pulled my lifeless body onto her lap and tilted my head back to begin mouth to mouth resuscitation. I immediately and violently sucked in an impossible amount of air and began hysterically screaming.

A child's horrified cries probably never sounded as sweet as mine did to Mom in that moment.

When the electricity took me down, I had swallowed my tongue which blocked my airway. Had Mom come out of the kitchen any later than she did, this story would have only been told by a mother who had been mourning for the past three decades. I'd be buried in some plot in Salt Lake City right now, and knowing me, my ghost would follow my folks from house to house, doing all sorts of weird shit to creep them out. I'm kind of a belligerent badass that way.

But, once again, I didn't die. And I am for some reason here to tell the tale myself. A tale that I don't remember, if I'm being honest. I also don't remember running into traffic and being saved by angels.

Yet the stories were told so many times throughout my younger life that they have become *real* memories to me. It was I, that at some point, decided what kind of car it was that stopped miraculously. My parents never have made mention of it that I know of. I think I decided exactly how far away the car was. I decided how busy the intersection was. It may have even been me that decided who was holding my hand just before it happened. It was my imagination that made the curtains brown and yellow the day I was electrocuted. It was in my imagination that Mom felt I must already be dead when she pulled me onto her lap. There are dozens of other details that I remember from those two incidents, all which fill in the gaps of an implanted memory.

The rest of my stories in this book are all real memories to me. They start later in my life, when my mind could actually make more sense of the day to day, and really learn more abstract lessons from such simple events.

The reason I share these two earlier stories is because I find two things about them to be overly fascinating (well, that and they tell me it's always good to start off a book with something gut-wrenching or dramatic).

First, I cannot think of any deep lessons that I personally learned. I have had other near death experiences since then, and the life lessons I've absorbed through each of them have been plentiful. Yet, the best I can come up with looking back at these is "don't let go of your kid next to a busy intersection," and "replace household fixtures that have frayed power cords."

But those aren't my lessons; those are my parents' lessons. They are simply tips that I can think about and implement in my own life as a father, nothing more. I would be willing to bet that my parents learned much more significant lessons than that in both situations.

Second, I have a difficult time feeling any of the natural humor that certainly *had* to exist in those experiences, even if it didn't surface until much later. If life has taught me anything, it's that even our worst experiences and heavy trials are laced with and surrounded by things we can laugh at, *if* we are willing to let go of the need to appear perfect or to be martyrs, and actually laugh at ourselves.

I *attempted* to insert at least a little humor into my narration of the stories above, but it felt insincere to me and so for the most part, I left it as was: as factual as it could be based on what I've been told. When I compare that humor to the reflective humor I sincerely felt as I wrote the rest of this book, it almost seems like humor shouldn't be included in the above stories at all.

I bring this up because I really hope that this book pushes people to look at their *own* life stories and search for both the humor and the lessons that exist within *all* of them. I think it is safe to say that as we do that, we can look at both the lessons, and the degree of humor we are able to find, and determine whether our stories are our own or if they ultimately belong to someone else.

The stories above, just like the lessons, actually belong to my parents. They don't belong to me. The stories that fill the rest of these pages are mine, and I cherish them the way I treasure a dear friend. I laugh with them the way I'd laugh with a dear friend. And I contemplate them, the way I'd look back and recount the past with a dear friend as well.

Was I saved by miracles as a child? I don't know, and I can't say. Like I said, I can't remember it. I only have the incomplete stories and perspective of others to bank on.

As one who struggles to accept religion and a defined definition of God, I do have to ask myself *why* certain unexplainable things happen. Is everything actually a coincidence, or are some of the details of our lives guided and nudged more than I'd like to give them credit for? And do we as human beings exaggerate our own memories, even to ourselves, and use our stories to strengthen our own faith and promote our beliefs to others?

Again, I don't know and I can't say.

All I can do is tell my own stories, and see the biggest miracle of my life for what it is: I have been able to laugh and learn through, or after, every difficult thing I have ever been through.

Everything in this book is true according to my own memory (minus the frequent ridiculous and obvious exaggerations). I have not made anything up. Perhaps some tiny details have implanted in my mind over the years just like the color of the drapes or the make of the car in my stories above, but I have not purposefully invented anything. It is also not lost on me that these are all from my own perspective, and the details may vary greatly had the same stories been told by others who were there. Like an old wise colleague of mine used to say, "no matter how thin, there are always two sides to every pancake."

And isn't that what makes anyone's life stories so great? There are almost always at least two versions to be heard, sometimes more, and sometimes they all greatly contradict the others.

The best stories are those passionately told around a dinner table, only to have another family member or friend lovingly cry out, "that's not how it happened!" or "you left out the most important parts!" at the top of their lungs while immediately jumping into an even greater version of the exact same story.

Every life story you or I tell is a living, breathing, always evolving memory, and the method I used to decide which of my stories to share was simple. I believe that any memory which constantly surfaces, no matter how big or how small, is attached to a greater lesson. And so over the course of days, I sat down and listed out every memory (no matter how seemingly unimportant it was) that constantly has surfaced for me throughout my life. Then, I itemized the greater lessons learned in each of them.

My list ended up *really* surprising me. Not only was it much longer than I anticipated (I only included a fraction of them in this book), but I also saw very quickly just why I have been shaped the way I have. I easily saw which of them have influenced what I now believe, and I uncovered so many factors that have made me feel certain ways about so many things as I age. I suddenly could see why I act and react to so many different stimuli the way I do. I understood why I have great compassion toward certain people, and immediate annoyance or apathy towards others. I was reminded of important lessons that I've let fade with time. I was also able to finally understand some of the greater lessons that I had never put into formed thought.

When I was done with that exercise, I chose some of the memories that I thought fit together nicely, changed the names of almost everyone, and got to work on this book.

If you purchased this book, I can only assume you got suckered into buying it by some four-toed carnie selling used books and magic toad potions to finance his personal drug habit.

You *probably* should have bought the potion.

But thank you for buying (or borrowing, or finding) the book.

I hope you are at least entertained and absorbed enough with the following chapters that you don't stand up in your favorite coffee shop and vehemently rant about the bleepity bleep portion of your life you'll never get back because of this bleepity bleep author who's so bleepity bleep mind-numbing and dull.

If you do find yourself in this situation, do us both a favor and toss my book into a recycle bin as you change modes and quietly exit. Maybe someone with time to waste on my ridiculous stories will fish it out and read it. Maybe a homeless person will use its pages to start a small trash fire in the alley and stay warm. Maybe some impossibly old matron will use it to smack her impossibly older husband for telling the barista that her boobs don't look perky enough to be as young as she claims she is. Maybe some guy wearing biker shorts will look down and see that he dripped pee on his own leg while using the urinal, and use my book to wipe himself clean. At worst, that hotty you've been eyeing across the shop will think you're the good kind of human for recycling.

Don't Do *This*. It's Bad.

Right about the time when my body was on the verge of transforming from pasty-white scrawny child to pudgy awkward beginning-to-pimple preteen, Dad called my brother and me into his den and sat us down for "the talk." My brother Eric was seven. I was almost nine.

Dad was a man you learned to say yes to. He never demanded a *yes sir* from any of his ten children, but was more interested in complete and immediate compliance in all things. There was no debating anything. Ever. And if you tried, you'd immediately have to run and grab the paddle or a shoe and then bend over (often with cheeks exposed) for a solid whoopin'. He towered almost six and a half feet off the ground, which, when you're a kid is *way* the hell up there. When he would get mad, his eyes would bulge from their sockets, he'd pierce his lips together, and he'd give you a look and a quiet huff that said, "say one more word; I dare you."

But Dad was also often a jovial man. He played with his kids. He cherished his kids. And he did his best to always teach his kids how to find the lessons in what life was trying to teach them. He was faithful in his marriage and in his church. From what I know, he never permitted a thought to alter him otherwise. He would laugh with you. Wrestle you. Massage your legs when they cramped up in the middle of the night, and as he did, he'd close his eyes ever so, he'd half-grin, and he'd tell you it was going to be all right. And because he was a man of his word, you believed him.

But the day he brought Eric and me into his den, he was neither serious nor jovial. He wasn't scary, yet he wasn't inviting. His shrunk back and uneven shoulders said he didn't want to be there. His tensed eyes said he *really* didn't want to be there. Up until that point, I never knew that anything could be awkward for my father.

He grabbed a pad of graph paper and told us to come stand at his desk.

"This is a penis, you already know that," he said as he doodled a cartoon with male genitals. He drew a ball sack hanging from the guy and explained to us what testicles and scrotums were. He explained to us that our balls would probably get bigger soon. My brother and I kept shooting awkward smirks at each other.

Then Dad got *really* uncomfortable as he started drawing the outline of a woman's body. He didn't get very far with it, just an outline of her head and shoulders. Suddenly he crumpled it up and told us to sit down. I think he realized all too quickly that he couldn't draw a naked woman for his young boys. Drawing a dude's junk had been difficult enough.

My brother and I sat down on the chairs he kept against the wall, uncomfortable and entertained all at once. Wanting to giggle. Deathly afraid to be paddled if we did. And then he made things really awkward by bringing Mom into the conversation. "You know how your mom is a woman and she has breasts?" We nodded. I don't think I knew what breasts were. "She also has another private part that boys don't have. It's called a..."

He trailed off discomfited, and switched gears to now leave Mom out of it. "Girls," he continued, "all girls in the whole world have what's called a vagina."

I can't speak for my brother, but at that point I definitely had no idea what the hell he was talking about. I'd seen my little sisters running around buck naked enough to know they didn't have penises, but I'd never heard of this weird vagina thing before.

Then Dad clarified that he was talking about "the peaches." Peaches are what we called vaginas in our home, a term that gives me the serious willies as an adult. I couldn't help but snicker at it that day, though. I didn't even know why winkies (our family word for penises) and peaches were so funny, I just knew they were. It probably had to do with the fact that everyone seemed to get so awkward about them, including Dad in that moment.

And, with a new semi-accurate understanding of who had what between their legs, we then learned about… *sex*.

I was appalled. I was mortified. I was absolutely disgusted.

A man does what now? To a woman?! *And you've done this to* Mom!? *And she* let *you?* My thoughts were racing as he explained the ins and outs of it all. Pun intended.

"It's how babies are made."

I looked at him in complete disbelief. *Not true. Definitely not true. Mom told me, God puts babies in your tummy. They certainly don't come because you stick your winkie into a girl's peaches. Uh uh. I won't believe it. I can't believe it.*

Still, I didn't debate and I didn't argue. I just shot occasional glances at my brother to silently ask him if he was also hearing this absurdity. He shot me back more of the same.

Dad then went on to try and explain sperm and eggs, and how that was the way each of us were made.

In a matter of minutes, I went through all the stages of grief. I had lost my innocence, and I had to deal with that. It started with denial, then moved to anger, then reflection as I thought about all the times I knew my parents must have been getting it on after sending us to bed early, and finally reluctant acceptance.

Eventually Dad finished. He didn't speak for some time, and suddenly he sighed very loudly and sat back into his creaky office chair. It was the kind of sigh that people sigh when they've just accomplished a really huge task. Or maybe it was the kind of sigh that people sigh when they come out unscathed from something that was really scary. But it wasn't enough of a sigh to dismiss us. No, we knew something else was coming. He had something else to tell us. And whatever it was, terrified him.

"There's one other thing that's really important," he finally said. I think his eyes may have been closed. Or at least mostly closed. His voice softened. And barely audibly, he held up the extended index finger of his left hand, and made a circle with the thumb and fingers of his right hand. He then began to vigorously stroke his left finger up and down.

"Never. Do. This. It's bad."

I had no idea why it was bad, but the way he told us it was bad, we knew it was *really* bad. Neither one of us said anything. We just nodded once again in compliance.

Dad grunted and nodded as well. He stood up from his chair without saying another word about it. "Go help your mother set the table," he said. And he has never since said a single educational word to us about sex that I can remember.

Eric and I both began giggling and then disappeared to do as we were told.

And I can honestly tell you that neither one of us ever made that appalling hand gesture for at least the next decade.

Neither one of us *ever* held out one index finger and then stroked it vigorously with the circled thumb and fingers of our other hand.

But later on I certainly did masturbate, which in case you missed it, was what Dad was *endeavoring* to tell us not to do. Yes, only years after that educational evening in his den, I was masturbating frequently and with wild abandon. In fact, to catch me in a window in which masturbating hadn't just happened or wasn't about to happen was probably rare indeed.

But I *never* made that hand gesture. Ever. Not to anyone. Not to my brother. Not even to myself. Just thinking about the hand gesture made me feel dirty and evil inside, and if I'm being honest, it still does to this day.

Dad had gotten his point across, and he had installed the fear into us that he set out to install. It just happened that the message got a bit distorted in translation.

"Never. Do. This. It's bad."

Now all these years later, I sometimes think back to that awkward evening in Dad's den, and I understand the real lesson to be had in all of it.

When we have something *important* to say or teach others, we shouldn't beat around the bush with it (again, pun intended). People won't get it. This applies to parenting our kids as much as it applies to our friendships, our social interactions, and our workplaces.

To be effective communicators we need to be bold about what we want others to know. We need to be non-apologetic. And we need to be clear.

It does nobody any good if we worry so much about making things awkward that nobody ever knows what we wanted or what we were working toward in the first place. It does nobody any good if we worry about being so politically correct that we alienate those who don't connect with such thinking. It does nobody any good if we try to phrase our ideas and words in such a way that they'll never offend anyone. And even worse, sometimes when we do this, we send the *wrong* message to others.

If I mean x, I need to say x. I don't need to give a complicated formula with lots of other variables, and expect others to solve for x when I already know damn well what x is and I want them to understand x. This is what I learned from Dad that night more than anything else, even if it took another decade or two and a willy rubbed raw to finally sink in.

Awkward First Love

Outside my family's home on Elwood Way, there was a mailbox. There was absolutely nothing special about this mailbox. It was made of tin, slightly rusted, and more than a little wobbly. The numbers of our address were clumsily attached to its side. It looked like every other mailbox on the street.

I was ten years old. I only got mail to that mailbox once every year in the form of a birthday card from my grandparents. Every other day I would watch Mom or Dad carry in a big stack of mail and sort through it, always hoping they'd, just one time, stop in the middle of their routine, look up, and enthusiastically say, "one for you, Danny!" It never happened.

Of course, now that I'm an adult, I understand why they never had enthusiastic smiles at all. Mail sucks. Almost everything that comes is either a piece of paper saying "PAY ME!" or an advertisement saying "GIVE US YOUR MONEY!" But as a kid, I thought that just about every envelope they were opening was as wondrous as a birthday card, and I really wanted in on some of it.

Then one day, Kari, a little sandy blonde girl who lived down the street, stuck something in that mailbox. For me. It was a plain white envelope, and across the top it just said, "To Danny."

Mom and Dad never saw that envelope. They never had the chance. In the middle of the day, my older sister came bounding into my room and interrupted me while I worked on a jigsaw puzzle. I was *really* good at jigsaw puzzles. Like really, really good at them. I could do a 1,000-piece puzzle before I was even old enough to start getting complaints about B.O. But seriously, this isn't about me. Or my amazing jigsaw puzzle skills. Or the fact that I could somehow do puzzles that were practically solid colors. Stop thinking how awesome I am for that. This is about Kari, and the envelope she left in my mailbox.

Anyway, Tomi Ann came bounding into my bedroom. She had a *huge* smile smeared across her face. That wasn't like Tomi Ann. Not when it came to her and me. We were mortal enemies more often than not, and our entire co-existence as children could be summed up in two words: eternal tattling. Yet there she was, standing above me, glowing. "Go check the mailbox! There's something in there for you!" she screeched.

I'm pretty sure I was at the mailbox before she finished her sentence.

I yanked the front open, stuffed my hand inside, and pulled out the white envelope.

Suddenly that mailbox wasn't just some rusty old tin clunker. It was my deliverer from all things mundane and ordinary.

To Danny

My heart doubled its pace. Next to the words were two little colorful hearts. *What was this? Who would send me this?* My sister was standing over me, eagerly waiting for me to tear into it. "Open it!" she demanded. I never paused to wonder why she was taking so much interest in it.

I ripped open the flap, and pulled out a bright yellow sheet of paper.

"Dear Danny, I like you a lot. Tomorrow you will get a present from me."

There was no signature. No identifying marks of any kind. It was a love note from a Jane Doe.

Tomi Ann began grilling me to see if I had any idea who might have sent it. I had no clue. I had no friends who were girls. I had no crushes on any girls. I had no memory of even talking to a girl. Ever.

But I fell in love with the sender of that letter immediately. It could have been from an eighty-year-old cat lady and I would have devoted my life and heart to her in that moment. I had never experienced butterflies or a rush of excitement the way I did right then, and that night I didn't get much sleep as I waited for my surprise the next day. What would it be? Money? Some Garbage Pail Kid trading cards? My own Atari? A king-sized Kit Kat bar?

The next afternoon, Tomi Ann snuck Kari through my house and in to my mother where Kari asked if she could be allowed into my bedroom to put something on my bed. Mom told her sure, go ahead. And according to Kari, she insisted, "you can like him, but nothing more."

Geez Mom, way to blow my first chance at a hot make-out.

As if.

I was ten. I was still a solid year away from puberty. To me, "something more" involved making weird hand gestures taught to me by my dad, remember?

And it didn't matter, I was already in love before I even walked in and saw the next sheet of paper laying across my pillow. Taped to the paper was a Now & Later candy. Next to the word Now it said, "I'll love you." Next to the word Later, it said, "I'll marry you."

I had finally found my forever sweetheart. I would marry this woman. But who it was I still didn't know. There was no name attached to it. Not even a hint to help me solve the riddle.

I turned around to see my older sister peeking around the corner into my room. I looked at her with wide eyes and she misread that as an invitation to come in. "It's from Kari!" she screamed and snorted all at once in her excitement. "She's in love with you!" Kari was one of Tomi Ann's best friends.

We made our way outside, sat down on the porch together, and made a plan for how we were going to make this union come about. Sitting next to my sister that day is one of my best childhood memories. It was one of the few times we found ourselves on the same team instead of at each other's throats. She was genuinely excited for me and determined to have a hand in something happy coming to me.

And boy, did the happy times come.

The next two weeks were spent back and forth between Kari's house and mine. We built things in the sandbox. We made cookies together. We jumped on her trampoline at least daily. We hunted for snakes together. We were in love.

But looking back at it, the fun and happy memories are very dim for me while two other memories have always loomed largely in my mind.

No matter how much fun we were having, we said almost nothing to each other. As in, ever. I bet most days, less than thirty words were exchanged between the two of us.

"Wanna look for snakes?"

"Sure."

Then we'd look for snakes. In silence.

"Wanna make cookies?"

"Sure."

Then we'd make cookies. In silence except to discuss measurements or ingredients.

"Wanna go behind The Chicken Lady's house and smoke pot?"

"Sure."

Okay, that last one didn't happen, but if it did, we would have done that in silence as well. I mean, we really liked each other, but we had no idea how to actually *talk* to each other. And yes, there really was a woman around the corner who we all called The Chicken Lady. She would come out onto her porch when we passed by for school, and she'd just start bocking loud chicken sounds at us. She was terrifying.

And as strange as the no-talking memory has always been for me, there has been a much stranger one. I had a *giant* wart on the palm of my left hand.

I hated that wart. I *loathed* that wart. And I did everything in my power to hide that wart from my first love. And that's probably why I even remember so much of what we did together at all. I remember jumping on the trampoline because I remember she wanted to hold hands while we did it, and I had to always make sure she held my right hand so that she wouldn't see it. I remember making cookies because I remember purposefully grabbing measuring cups and tablespoons with my right hand while my left hand stayed shoved in my pocket. I remember searching for snakes because I remember holding the snakes in such a way that she would see only the snake and not the grotesque disfigurement on my body.

I just *knew* that my wart would be the end of our love affair. I didn't think she would ever be able to look past it once she knew it existed. I thought she would be disgusted by it, and I didn't want this girl I loved to disappear. Not over a wart.

Two weeks after our relationship started, it ended. I don't know why. I think one of us moved. Or we just forgot that we were in love. Who knows.

What I do know is that I've thought about that wart over the years. I've seen how that dynamic has shown up in my other relationships. I've seen it show up so often in the relationships of others. We meet someone, we fall for them, and we're so scared of losing them that we actively hide our warts.

Okay, that just sounds gross. When grown-ups have warts, they're usually on their no-no bits, but you get what I'm saying.

We don't show others our flaws. We hide those parts of us that we think the other person will never accept. We do everything we can to appear as perfect as we can for as long as we can.

But that's not love.

What I had with Kari wasn't actually love at all. It was excitement mixed with friendship. I know, because now I know what love actually is. Now that I'm older and I've had lots and lots of relationships (I'm still really good at jigsaw puzzles, by the way), I know that love is never real unless its foundation is a real one. Love that is founded on some weird and fake guise of perfection will always fail.

Which is why I now show my "warts" as quickly as possible to the people who come into my life. Some people can't handle my warts. And that's okay, too. I'd rather hold hands with someone and think about the fun we're having than hold hands with them while constantly fearing what will happen if they learn the truth that is me.

I Would Never Do That

We're going to talk about this whether it's awkward or not.

The discovery of masturbation is probably the most universally life altering occurrence in a young man's life. It's the golden spike in the ground that divides boyhood from manhood and starts each kid down the path that will lead to the most stupid, idiotic, and glorious decisions of his life.

I like to believe that thinking and feeling is a skill that men have to increasingly master just as they have to learn proper communication skills, parenting skills, or Kung Fu skills.

I believe there are four organs that we each eventually (hopefully) learn to use to both think and feel, and it is only when we effectively can use all four together that we become truly balanced individuals.

When we are children we generally only use one. Our brains. *Anyone* can use their brain. It is only later in life that we will progress one step at a time to use the correct parts of our brains as well as the other three thinking and feeling organs, starting next with our penises, then progressing to our stomachs, and finally, if we evolve enough, we will start thinking and feeling with our hearts.

When I was still little enough to fit into a standard bathtub with Eric, the two of us used to lie down on our bellies side by side, and slide back and forth in the tub, rubbing our nethers on the smooth porcelain below. We were little and this was fun for two big reasons.

One, we could get a pretty good sloshy wave going on both ends of the tub as we went, and two, we'd get boners.

There was nothing sexual about it. Both of us were still years away from puberty when we finally couldn't fit in the same tub together. And I don't know if my brother kept going with his slishing and sloshing fun when he went solo, but I sure as hell did. Sure, boners weren't as funny when you were by yourself, but they were still pretty damn comical.

And when I was eleven years old, my innocent fun in the bathtub one afternoon ended with surprisingly explosive results. It sounds cliché, but I really do remember it like it was last week. I was on my belly, humming me some Neil Diamond, rubbing my willie up and down the length of the tub as I so often did, and suddenly what never really felt like anything at all started feeling *really* good.

What the…

I stopped humming and increased my pace. Back and forth. Back and forth. The more I did it the better my penis felt. And then, out of freaking *nowhere*, the danged thing had some sort of wonderful spasm, and my body clenched up against my will, I held my breath against my will, I clamped my eyes shut against my will, and I suddenly felt something shoot out of me and into the bubbly water.

Once it had passed, I let myself gasp a lungful of air. My breath was now even heavier than it had been all those years chasing the other kids around at soccer practice. I held myself perfectly still in the bathtub, looked down into the water, and shook my head in disbelief.

What was that? I just thought over and over.

I felt no guilt. No hesitation. No disgust. Nothing bad. I would learn later on that in my Mormon family, masturbation was a big no no. But at that point, I just thought the sin meant not stroking your own index finger in some perverse manner. Dad had never made mention of anything as glorious as this when he gave us the sex talk.

Once my breathing had calmed, I gave it another go. Nothing this time. So I drained the tub.

I dried off, and prayed as hard as I could that the next time I got in the bathtub I could find a way to repeat what had just happened. It was, after all, the most magical thing I had ever felt.

And whatever god I was praying to answered those prayers. The next time it took no time at all for me to get that magic feeling going again. And, just like the time before, I exploded into the water with what felt like the intensity of a fire hose and the magic of a unicorn sliding down a rainbow into a pot of fucking gold.

I started doing it often and with wild abandon after that. I learned that there was more than one way to get that lovin' feeling. In fact, there were lots of ways and not all of them had to be in the bathtub. Months into it, and probably hundreds of masturbations later, I had never once felt guilt. I had never once felt like I was disgusting. I had never once felt that it was wrong. After all, how could something so wrong feel so right?

After accidentally telling us not to stroke our own fingers in his attempt to teach us not to masturbate, I suppose Dad thought the lesson had been learned, he was done, and he never again needed to teach us not to charm our one-eyed snakes; because of that, he never brought it up again. My friends, on the other hand, they were a different story altogether.

My friends were *all* raised as Mormons just as I was, and looking back at the often hilarious conversations we used to have as we went through puberty, I'd guess that their dads did a more thorough job of explaining masturbation and teaching them how awful, and sinful, and *wrong* it was.

The first time masturbation was ever brought up, I was at my best friend's house. We were laying on his basement floor watching TV and suddenly he piped in, "dude, I seriously dare you to masturbate, right now."

I had no idea what masturbation was. I'd never heard that word. "What are you talking about? What's that?" I replied.

"Whatever. You know what it is" he demanded between laughs. I assured him I didn't. He laughed again. "It's when you rub your wiener until it spits jiz."

He needed to offer no further explanation. I now had a name for my magic little secret. Did that mean other boys did this masturbate thing too? Did that mean it was something *grown-ups* knew about?

The way he was daring me to do it made it sound like it was wrong or iniquitous. After all, we only ever *dared* each other to do things that we could potentially be busted for. Jumping up and down on the trampoline naked. Stealing stuff. Shooting birds with his BB gun. And now, apparently, masturbating.

"Is masturbating bad?" I asked. "It's not like I do it or anything, I'm just wondering." I knew the answer. I didn't want to hear it. I knew I needed to hear it.

Again my best friend laughed. This time a lot more uncomfortably. "Of course it's bad. It's like the worst thing you can do. That's why it's a dare."

And… just like that, my new suspicions about the act were confirmed.

Suddenly I felt like the world's biggest piece of shit. I thought back to all the hundreds of times I had masturbated to that point.

God must hate me.

"Well, I don't masturbate. I'm not going to do *that*," I told him matter of factly. "Why don't you do it."

His laugh turned into a nervous twitter. "I don't do it either. No way. I just wanted to see if you'd do it. That's disgusting and I'd never do it."

We both just lay in silence after that, the TV blaring in front of us. And we never talked about masturbation again in the three years we remained best friends.

But from that night forward, I hated myself for this thing called masturbation.

And not in some feel bad for me, I'm going to be over-dramatic way. I literally *hated* myself for it. Mostly because I couldn't stop doing it.

Every time I finished masturbating, in that amazing ten minutes when I was thinking with my brain instead of my penis again, I would swear to myself, and to God, that I would never do it again. Ever.

And then twelve hours later, or twenty-four hours later if I was really trying hard, I'd have another go. I'd feel another wave of self-loathing when I was done. And I'd promise God that it was the *last* time it would happen. I meant it, too. Every fucking time.

The further I crept into my teenage years, the worse my guilt and self-abhorrence got. Other friends would talk about how they *never* would do it. They'd laugh about it. Rumors would spread that someone in the group was doing it, and every boy there would laugh and declare to the group that they'd *never* do such an awful thing. I would laugh and announce to the group that I also would never do that. Then I'd go home and start my masturbation/prayer cycle all over again, believing that I was the only kid in the world who couldn't stop beating off. I had no idea that they were all doing the exact same thing.

I learned a lot looking back at that. I learned that we each need to examine everything we have been taught is right or wrong and decide whether we actually believe it's right or wrong, or if someone else's beliefs are dictating our guilt to us.

I was *taught* that masturbation was wrong. Before someone told me it was bad, I did not think it was wrong at all. I didn't think it was dirty. I didn't think I was a misfit. I didn't think I was weak. I never once had a negative thought surrounding it.

I left the Mormon church when I was 30, and when I did, I had to really examine so many things that I was taught were wrong or forbidden, and decide if I really believed that they were wrong, or if I only believed it because I'd been told so many times that they were wrong by others.

And you know what? I found that I did agree with many of the things I was always taught. Stealing is wrong. Deceiving others is wrong. Skipping out on your family as a father is wrong. Killing people is definitely wrong.

But other things no longer felt wrong to me. Not when I looked into my own heart and began deciding what was right or wrong with *that* organ instead. Masturbation, to me, is not wrong. It can be, in fact, just as magical and *funny* as it was when I first discovered it. Drinking alcohol is not bad or wrong. Premarital sex is not bad or wrong. To *me*.

And when I started drinking occasionally, or having sex outside of marriage from time to time, or masturbating to relieve stress, I learned that the guilt I so often felt for "sinning" was all something that had been extrinsically placed into my thinking by others.

Coincidentally, I also learned that within each of those activities there is a line that, when crossed, the activity becomes wrong to me. Drinking for much more than a fun evening *feels* wrong to me. Drinking to eliminate sadness or anger *feels* wrong to me. Drinking irresponsibly *feels* wrong to me. Also, sex with someone I'm not interested in having something at least a little longer-term with *feels* wrong to me. Sometimes. Sometimes not. Masturbating while humming Neil Diamond definitely *feels* wrong to me. Barbara Streisand is much more appropriate. And yes, I have done it.

But my point is, I learned that every person (at some point in their lives) has to zoom out from their upbringing and examine their beliefs of right and wrong. Wrong and right is *so* different for everyone and every person needs to dissect every aspect of it and decide if they actually believe what they practice and preach.

When we are able to honestly do this, I believe we have finally evolved to think and feel with our hearts more than we do with our minds, our guts, or our sexual organs. And thinking and feeling with our hearts is the only way we will ever live lives that are completely ours and that are genuinely fulfilling and free.

Two Mile Walk of Shame

The allure was too much for a portly preteen whose friends were all speedily leaving him behind in the world of music.

13 CDs for the price of one. Or some ridiculous thing like that.

I flipped the glossy and colorful mailer front to back in my hand. I had snatched it out of the stack of mail Dad had brought in the night before. 13 compact discs for the price of one. Simply fill out the card and send it in, they'd mail me four of them, then I'd send in a payment for just one freaking CD and they'd mail me the other eight.

I flipped the advertisement front to back again. I opened it up for the hundredth time. Inside were dozens of the most popular albums available. I didn't know any of the music. I wasn't allowed to listen to much outside of Mom and Dad's light sounds radio station. But I recognized and had already circled the names of lots of them. My friends were always talking about them. They were always singing random songs with each other. They had written the names of some of these bands on the leather bottoms of their backpacks.

And I wanted in.

I *had* to have them.

At one point I had written Pearl Jam on the bottom of *my* backpack just to fit in and my best friend loudly called me out on it in front of everyone on the school bus. "You don't even know who Pearl Jam is!" he blurted.

"Yes I do! They're an awesome band!"

He pointed at my backpack and started forcefully laughing. Hard. "Name one song they sing. Name even one song! I bet you can't!"

I couldn't answer. Mortified, I slunk into my seat, clutched my backpack to my chest, and silently resented my parents *so* much for their strict music rules. I grew up on Bette Midler and The Carpenters. The coolest song I knew was *Cat's in the Cradle*. And believe me, my friends wouldn't have thought it was cool that I knew every word to Barbara Streisand's *Yentl* soundtrack, so I kept that one to myself.

Yes, I *needed* those CDs. My social life depended on it

I closed the mailer and studied it once more. I knew what I would have to do in order to get them.

Hidden deep in the back of Dad's middle desk drawer in his den was his checkbook. I'd seen Mom write out enough checks to know how they worked. Date. Amount. Amount written out again in longhand. Memo. Signature. Dad would never notice fifteen bucks gone missing. I had seen his John Hancock plenty of times. The CD company would have no idea the check was forged. It was fool proof.

With plan in place, I filled out the mailer under Dad's name and sent it on its way.

And, sure enough. 4-6 weeks later, a small box was sitting on the porch when I arrived home from school one afternoon. I snatched it up. "Columbia House." Yes! It was here. I shoved it under my sweatshirt, ran downstairs as fast as my chubby legs could carry me, eagerly yanked my Simon and Garfunkel CD out of my Discman, and spent the next three hours listening to the most awful sounding crap I had ever heard.

I'd never listened to music so obnoxious and harsh. Picking a melody out of *any* of it was a tedious task for my untrained ears.

But it didn't matter. I shoved every harsh thought about it to the back of my mind. It may have been awful crap, but it was the same awful crap that my friends were always talking about. Next time someone put me on the spot, I'd have all sorts of song titles ready to spew out at a moment's notice.

After listening to Pearl Jam, Nirvana, Pink Floyd, and Stone Temple Pilots for three days, I carried through on phase two of my plan, forged a check for what I owed, and sent it off. A couple weeks later I was painfully trying to like a brand new stack of albums and as I did, I thought over and over about that checkbook. It was the easiest thing I'd ever done. No repercussions. No sign of the sin. No having to answer to anyone. And from there I began thinking about all the things I could do with this new access to easy money.

I never got the chance to do it again though.

"Dan, come up here and talk to me and your mom." Dad yelled down to the basement a few days later. He sounded upset. And when Dad was upset, you didn't dawdle.

Dawdling earned you an extra smack or two with the paddle or one of his size 13 tennis shoes.

He was standing by the door to his den waiting for me with arms folded. As soon as I walked past him, he shut the door behind me. *That wasn't a good sign.* Mom was sitting tall in the stuffed floral chair in front of his desk. She was showing no emotion and didn't make eye contact with me. *That wasn't a good sign either.* He passed by me again and sat heavily into his large leather office chair. And then he just stared at me, his gaze centered on mine. He didn't say anything for some time. *That definitely wasn't a good sign.*

Finally, he spoke. Quietly. Not angrily. "Did you know that the bank sends me copies of all the checks I write?"

Oh crap. I shook my head slowly.

He kept his heavy stare centered on me. I looked away. "Come here and look at this."

Oh crap. Oh crap. Oh crap. Eight steps later I was standing by his side. He pulled out a copy of the check I had written.

"Did you do this?"

I was too young to die. I was too smart to deny it. I couldn't confess it with any amount of saving grace, either. Instead I broke down into a crying fit and word-vomited the truth about everything. I told him about the CDs. I told him about the check. I told him how hard it was to be the only kid who doesn't get to listen to cool music.

He just sat. And listened. Watching me intently. Absorbing it. Waiting for me to finish.

After my tearful confession, I waited for him to pass his judgment. Would I do dishes for a month? Would I be grounded for a year? Would I get the world record for hardest and longest butt whoopin' of all time?

Still he stared.

"Is there anything else you'd like to tell us?" He was looking deep into my soul now. He knew. He knew everything. He didn't just know about the CDs. He knew about the masturbation too. How he knew, I had no idea. But his eyes told me. And again, I broke down into even louder sobs.

"Not that I want to tell *you*," I said between blubs.

"Who do you want to tell?"

It was too late to turn back. "The Bishop." You see, Mormons are *supposed* to go confess to their assigned Bishop any time they masturbate. I had learned that much from my friends.

Dad's face never flinched. His eyes didn't bulge like they always did when he got angry. His lips didn't pierce. He didn't give me his look and his famous huff. Instead he took it face on. "Is it masturbation?"

This was the first time I remember literally wailing uncontrollably in my life. "YES!" I said through strings of slobber. I knew that I would be hated and loathed by my own parents now. I knew that I would never leave the house again. I knew that I might not even make it out of that room. The end of my world had officially come.

"You will bring me those CDs. You don't get to keep them. You'll also pay me back for those CDs. And if you ever forge another check, there will be much bigger consequences."

I looked at him through tear-filled eyes. *That's it? Really?* Then I realized why the CDs didn't matter. They were small potatoes compared to the real issue at hand. I had just told him that I masturbate. *End my life already if you're going to!*

I looked over at Mom. She was sitting in the chair and she was starting to blubber as hard as I was.

But he didn't end my life. Instead, he handed me the phone and said, "dial this number. You're going to make an appointment with Bishop Moon and tell him what you've been doing."

I took the phone and gave him a look that said, *please don't make me do this. Please.* He shot me a look in return that said, *do it. You do not want to see what happens if you don't.*

And so, I did. And I walked the two miles to the church the next day, and I sat in front of the Bishop, and I squeaked out to him that I was a dirty little masturbator. It was the *worst* and most consuming moment of my life to that point. I never hated my life and the church and my parents as much as I did sitting across from that man whom I barely knew, telling him that I liked to play with my tallywacker.

Of all the events that shaped me, I don't know that any in my life were more profound than this entire experience was. Even twenty years later, I think back to it often. I think back to what I learned in all of it. I think back to how it shaped the entire rest of my future relationship with my father and the church. I think back to what it taught me was most important and where to put my focus.

I gained more fear and more respect for Dad that day. I also learned that the way we react to our children when they make their biggest mistakes will sit with them far longer than the way we react to their more frequent and smaller ones.

In truth, I know I got spanked and paddled a *lot* as a child, but I really don't remember much of it at all because the spankings were tied to such silly events that were negligible in the long run.

But I promise you, a month never goes by that I don't for some reason think back to that night in his den and still feel a mixture of gratitude, anger, and resentment to this day.

He could have really made me pay the price for the stealing. In fact, he probably should have. Instead, he taught me that sometimes there is more power in remaining calm and letting a person's own guilt and conscience teach the lesson. I will always be thankful that he taught me that.

He also could have changed my entire life for the better from that point on. He could have made me feel normal and not disgusting or loathsome for my little naughty habit. Instead, he taught me that I needed to extrapolate the negative feelings of self-worth I was already experiencing and never be happy with myself so long as I couldn't control my devilish urges.

I already struggled to think I was lovable because of it before the whole thing happened. And from that point on as a teenager, I never felt like I had *any* goodness in me at all. I felt that both of my parents and every leader of the church could see straight into my soul and know exactly what I was doing into a tube sock at least daily, because from there on out, the masturbation only became more frequent. That building lack of self-respect and self-worth leaked into my schoolwork, my ability to socialize, and my ability to defend myself against bullies.

I think I will always be resentful to some degree that he handed me the phone and taught me that sometimes we should shame and guilt others into feeling worthless so that our own beliefs can sink in more properly.

That single evening in time has shaped more of my fathering strategies than anything else. Nearly every time I find myself having to delve out a consequence to my child, I find myself thinking back to those events and asking myself two questions. Does the punishment fit the crime? And does the punishment teach him or does it fill him with guilt? If the answer is that it fills him with guilt, I alter my tactics and I reword my strategies.

Whew.

Having said all that, I realize that this particular chapter got both long and heavy. And so, I shall end with a list of funny terms for male masturbation so that we can get back on track, and then I shall *hardly* bring up masturbation again in the rest of this book. Hopefully you're clever enough to understand that these chapters aren't really about masturbation all. But this list sure is.

Slap boxing the one-eyed champ
Beating off
Lighting the lamp post
Taming the snake
Choking the chicken
Loping your mule
Greasing the flagpole
Cranking the shank
Rubbing one out
Seasoning your meat
Working your willy
Buffing the banana
Milking the bull
Jimmying your joey
Jerking the Johnson
Backstroke roulette
And, my personal favorite: assault on a friendly weapon

Lick It.

Sweet summer was nearing, even if begrudgingly slow in its approach. I sat at my desk in Miss Peterson's class toward the end of fifth grade, watching the hands tick dangerously closer to 1:30.

I looked around the classroom. Other kids were also watching the clock, but the excitement on their faces was far different from the emotion I was trying to conceal. When the bell rang, they'd each run worry-free through those big red doors that led to the schoolyard. They'd excitedly begin their games of kickball and five-step. They'd round up their pals for buttball and soccer. They'd all go blow off some steam, run around, talk and laugh about wieners and boobs, be kids… All that fun stuff.

I looked over at Dawn, the ugliest girl in class. She'd be playing 4-square. The *loser*.

I knew where I'd be headed. Ever since Levi had violently flattened me against the turf during my first game of Five-Step, I wasn't taking any chances, that day especially. Earlier that morning, Levi and Miles had supplemented a rather painful sandwich slam (a particularly fun game they used to play in which they snuck up and struck me simultaneously from both sides) with a nice little threat on the side. "We're gonna find you today, Fat Ass."

I guess they had been looking for me recently. I had been praying that they hadn't, but I knew they had. Those two idiots never let up.

Levi was a skinny white kid with slightly wavy white hair. I remember him most for his always bloodshot and bulging eyes. When he talked, his voice was sharp and vicious. He had crooked yellow teeth and a permanent sneer plastered to his face. Levi had made it his goal to make my life as miserable as possible from the first day I showed up to that school. No, really. He did. He announced his goal to the entire class at recess one day. He was a class-A douchebag.

Miles was Levi's bitch. He was even fatter than I was, but he couldn't let me pass by in the halls or in class without snickering something at me about my weight. He had thick dark hair, a face absolutely covered in freckles, and would do *anything* Levi told him to do.

I would also like to add, with a silly little smile still, that in the years which followed, I liked to picture that they both were hiding tiny little dicks and really weird, wart covered nut sacks. I never saw their junk, but I'd bet a dollar against a donut hole that that's what it would have had to look like. I also often imagined that Miles had to wear a fluorescent pink bra to school and that Levi secretly enjoyed eating his own shit when no one was looking. Thoughts like that made thinking about that part of my past so much more bearable for me.

So, anyway, after class let out that late spring day, while the other kids zigged towards 30 minutes of freedom, I zagged straight to the little boys' room where I would wait it out for the bell to ring, giving me the cue that recess was over and I would once again be safe inside my classroom. It had been my daily routine for at least a week. I hated it, but I didn't have much of a choice, either. Every day that I didn't show up to recess, Levi and Miles were getting hungrier for a piece of me. To go outside now would be certain suicide. Not even ugly Dawn and the safety of the 4-square losers could save me at this point.

I locked myself into a bathroom stall and sat on the toilet behind me, my pants still pulled up. *Thirty minutes.* This bathroom had been an adequate hideout so far. I stared at the juvenile graffiti on the door in front of me. There were always so many wieners drawn on those doors. *Thirty minutes.* I looked at my watch. *Oh good. Only 29 minutes left.*

My mind drifted back to the game of Five-Step in which Levi had pile-driven me into the dirt. My best friend Jordan, standing on the other side of the field, stood from afar, watching it unfold. I wouldn't let the thought linger long, but he was embarrassed, maybe, to be my friend. Careful to not be seen with me at school. Come to think of it, he was always careful to not be seen with me at school. *He's not really your friend. Friends don't do that.* How much time had passed? Five minutes? I glanced at my watch again. Still 29 minutes left. *He is your friend. You play together every day after school.* Still 29 minutes. Time went so much slower locked in a pooper.

I stared at my watch and counted down from ten, willing the last digit to change. I counted down two additional times before it finally did. *Oh good. Only 28 minutes left.*

Suddenly the main door to the bathroom came bursting open. *Crap.* I lifted my legs into the air, praying that they were out of sight from whoever just entered.

"Hey Faaaaaat Aaaaaassss...." It was Levi. *Crap. Crap. Crap. I'm not in here. Leave me alone. Please God, don't let them see me.* "Hey Miles, look who I found." Levi's bloodshot eye suddenly appeared against the crack in the door. He stood there motionless, staring at me.

"Leave me alone, jerk. I'm going to the bathroom." *Please God. Please God. Please God.* Another eye, this one belonging to Miles, appeared and stared at me through the opposite crack. "What do you guys want?" I demanded, trying unsuccessfully to mask the debilitating fear that was now causing my heart to pound beyond its natural limits.

The eyes of both boys disappeared from view. "You thought you could hide from us?"

"I'm not hiding. I'm going to the bathroom."

"We'll always find you, Fatty."

I couldn't reply. The sound of Miles' foot kicking the stall door interrupted any attempt at rational thought. My fear turned into terror.

Levi and Miles began taking turns kicking or running at the door. *Stay closed. Stay locked.* It burst open. "Get out of here. Leave me alone! I didn't do anything to you guys."

I leapt from the toilet and attempted to push my way past them, but was forced backwards into the stall again. Miles kicked the back of my knees to buckle them while Levi began forcing my head toward the toilet seat. "Let me go," I said, this time barely audibly. If I didn't hold it together, I knew I wouldn't be able to stop myself from crying.

Miles successfully brought me to my knees while Levi continued to push my head closer to the commode. *I hate you. I hate you. I hate you.* My lips brushed the yellowed plastic toilet seat as I fought to keep my head hovered above it. Miles began helping Levi push my face further downward. My lips slowly smooshed into the disgusting seat below me.

"Lick it." Levi's voice as always so sharp and high.

I went limp. I couldn't fight against it anymore. "No," I grumbled as they began manually moving my head in a circular motion against the toilet. *God, please kill them.*

"Lick it."

"No."

One of them grabbed my hair and pulled. "We're not leaving until you lick it."

I could get out of this. I could scream. I could summon some adult to help me end this. *No, you can't.*

I was right. I couldn't. They'd just come after me harder and with increased regularity the next day. They'd make me pay for being a fink.

"Lick it."

I stuck the tip of my tongue against the toilet seat and quickly pulled it back in. "Okay, I licked it. Let me go."

"Sorry, it needs to be a real lick. Like, all the way across it."

"What's wrong with you guys?" I closed my eyes, trying to suppress my sudden urge to puke. *Dear God. Send somebody in here. Kill them. Do something. Please.*

"Do it and we'll leave you alone to sit in here on your fat ass and cry like a little baby."

Don't do it. There's probably crap and pee all over this thing. Don't do it. You can get out of this.

No, you can't. Just lick it and get rid of them.

I extended my tongue and swiped it across the full length of the toilet seat as I simultaneously gagged on the vomit that was now working its way up.

"Try hiding from us again. I dare you," Levi said as the four hands holding me down finally released me. I didn't look up. I simply rested my forehead on the toilet and listened as they ran from the bathroom.

Laughing.

Congratulating each other.

Celebrating.

After their voices had disappeared down the hall and through the big red doors, I stood and walked to the sink. *Don't cry. Don't cry.* A large tear emerged and rolled down my right cheek. *Do... not... cry.*

I washed my mouth out as best I could and looked at my watch. *Only 24 minutes to go.*

Now, I don't tell you this story to get pity, or to have you hate Levi and Miles. I tell you this story because I want you to understand what school was like for me with these two meatheads *always* around. Their ugly bullying would have its ups and downs in severity, but it lasted from fifth grade all the way until I graduated high school.

School was not a fun or safe experience for me. I never *hated* anyone as much as I hated these two guys.

I spent most of my post high school life trying to bury any memory I had of them at all. My body would instantly chill and my stomach would clench at a single thought of Levi's eyes or Miles' chubby fists. They took away a huge piece of who I was and who I could have been growing up. I lost my confidence, my will to thrive, and *so* much of my life to them. I didn't think I could ever forgive them for that.

But then, thanks to the miracle of Facebook, all of that changed.

They each independently contacted me a few years ago and told me how sorry they were for everything they had done. We agreed to all meet up, we actually hugged, we cried, and we became three of the best friends from then on out. Levi and Miles both talked it over and agreed to let me kick them in the nethers as hard as I could and then we'd call it even and let go of the past. I approved of this fabulous plan and I actually kicked Levi so hard that his nut severed. He admitted that he deserved it, and we all...

Oh crap. There I went fantasizing again. None of that was true. But Facebook did fundamentally change the way I looked at my two tormentors in general.

A few years ago, I was flipping through my yearbook and I came across Levi's photo. I stared at it for a moment, wondering how I could have such a physically disturbing reaction to it even all these years later. That led to thinking about everything they'd put me through, and eventually I really started to wonder what they looked like now. Were they even alive? Did they have good lives or shitty lives?

I first typed in Levi's name. He immediately popped to the top of the search results thanks to our many mutual friends. The face that greeted me was a grown-up version of the same face that never left me alone those seven years. His eyes were still strained and red. His hair was still almost pure white. He still had that permanent scowl. And... He looked *sad*. He looked *really* sad.

I scrolled though his photos. He only had two of them posted the entire time he had been on Facebook. In one photo he was holding his little daughter. In the other he was alone. In both photos, he reeked of sadness. I don't know a better way to explain it.

I looked at those two photos for the longest time, processing what that meant to me. Then I searched for Miles. He also immediately showed up at the top of the search.

If I didn't know it was him, I wouldn't have recognized him. He had probably gained 200 lbs. since the last time I saw him in high school. He had a single low-resolution photo on Facebook that he had posted years before. I checked recently. It still hasn't changed. In that photo, he also looked worn, and sad, and beaten down by life.

When I saw that photo, I had no choice but to forgive both of my bullies. Immediately and without need for an apology or severing kick to the nut sack.

All snarky fantasy aside, seeing a tiny glimpse of their current lives all these years down the road made me realize just how much worse these two guys must have had it than I ever did. Something about those images made me intrinsically understand that bullies are almost always created by other bullies.

We have a bullying problem in our schools, that's no big secret. Many great programs have been created to combat it and to fight it. Still, I can't help but think that so much time and effort is going toward fighting it and not toward solving it.

I learned that day on Facebook that bullies don't need people to fight with them. They need people to love them. We must learn to see past their outward actions and do what we can to see their internal battles if we are ever to change those individuals.

Whatever was happening outside of school to both of those boys had to have been so much worse than the horrible actions they were bringing into the school. They were simply passing along the abuse and torment they were receiving elsewhere. I was simply caught in the crosshairs. I have no doubt about that.

I also have no proof of this except what I can see in their eyes both now and when I remember those eyes from my past. There was never *anything* but pain in them. Twenty years later there is still nothing but pain in them.

I was one of the lucky ones who made it out of that and eventually took over my own life and found happiness, but I promise you it was a really bumpy road to do so. Much of what I've written in this book is evidence of that.

By the looks of it, my bullies didn't make it out. And that truly makes me sad. It makes me want and wish with all of my heart that someone would have really put their arms around those boys and helped them know that they were wanted and loved. I can't help but think that doing so would have helped both them *and* me.

Roxy

And now, a short and pointless little story from a different time in my life, with an even more pointless moral attached to it. The year: 2004.

A few years into my first marriage, we had a pet Boxer with beautiful fawn and white markings, long powerful legs, a short stubby nose, and eyes that were so warm they could melt snow in December. Roxy was by far the favorite of all the dogs I ever owned.

To say that she was high-energy would be like saying Louis Armstrong was a great musician. It's true, but it's not nearly true enough.

If Roxy didn't get substantial daily exercise, she would bounce around the house, completely unable to control herself, and knock over everything with which she came into contact. If we valued our stuff at all, we had no choice but to keep her exercised.

As a big fat guy who looked at exercise the same way Bob Ross probably looks at skateboarding (it just isn't going to happen), there was no way I was going to go out and give her the five miles or so of running she needed every day to chill the hell out. So, we'd use a 30-foot leash and my wife would sit on the tailgate of our SUV while I drove in circles around the nearest school parking lot 60 or 70 times with Roxy running in tow. She loved every minute of it. When it was over, she'd calmly mosey around the house the rest of the day like a normal, good dog.

Some days we couldn't take her on a run for one reason or another. I didn't mind so much. We'd play tug of war and wrestle until we were worn out. Then we'd *both* calmly mosey around the house the rest of the day like normal, good dogs.

Roxy had this favorite tug of war toy. It was a thick orange and white rope with frayed knots tied in both ends. She'd get hold of one end and you could not pull hard enough to yank it out of her mouth. Her jaws were so powerful and stubborn, I would sometimes lift her off the ground by the rope and carry her over my shoulder just for fun. She'd dangle there like a sack of yams. If I ever won tug-of-war, it was because she let me win not because I actually won. It was rare that she would do that for me.

But that wasn't enough for Roxy. If she felt that she wasn't winning fast enough, without letting go of her side of the rope, that dog would swing around and straddle the arm I was holding the rope with between all four of her legs. If I was on the floor, this was no big deal. If I was on the couch, it always left my face about four inches from her exposed butt hole.

I'm telling you right now, I don't care how much you love your dog, you don't want that right in your face. Ever. Or maybe you do, weirdo.

Anyway, one day we were having a particularly brutal war with the rope and she had straddled my arm as she sometimes did. Her ass was in my face like it so often was. And then it happened.

Pshshshshpshhsshshshshshshpshshpshhh.

It was long. It was steamy. It was hot. And it hit me right in the face with the gentleness of a wooing lover. The smell, on the other hand, hit me the way a third degree black belt would hit a stack of bricks. Impossibly fast, accurate, and with incredible power.

I felt the blood vessels in my eyes immediately tighten, and my eyes began to water.

I didn't breathe it in, and yet it was somehow saturating my nostrils and lungs anyway.

My stomach threatened to return my lunch back up to me.

And I let go of the rope.

She had won, yet again.

Pointless moral of the story: nothing pleasant will ever happen when you put your face next to an excited dog's ass.

And with that, we'll get back to it...

Sweat, Blood, & Smears

Two years after my first love disappeared like a silhouette into the rolling credits of a silent-era romance movie, and my Jabba the Hutt-sized wart was nothing but a faint and insulting memory, and I had officially hit puberty as was evidenced by those extra-long baths I *needed* to sneak off and take two or three times every day, I entered... The Boy Scouts.

The Boy Scouts gave me all sorts of exciting opportunities as a young ever-fattening lad. I'll never forget that first year when we were getting ready for Boy Scout summer camp and my next door neighbor, who happened to be a doctor, volunteered to give our whole troop physicals *for free!* Why no one ever questioned that is beyond me.

That physical was my first major public humiliation that I can recall. All twelve of us stood in a line together, in the same room, dropped our drawers, and one at a time, the doctor sat on his wheelie-chair, and felt our nuts. "Turn your head and cough." We all know the routine. As he came to me, I was praying that there wasn't some evidence of my new love for baths. I mean, what if all that "cleaning" going on in the bathtub was easy to spot by a trained medical professional? Luckily, after I gave a small grunt, he didn't say anything and moved on to the next kid. I was happy to pull my drawers back up and hide my pudgy thighs and newly sprouting pubes.

My next major humiliation would come early that summer, also before Scout camp.

Where we lived, there were a *lot* of mountains. And a lot of mountains means a *lot* of hiking trails. Let me share an equation with you. Boy Scouts + mountains + hiking trails = lots of chances for chubby little preteens to learn about the cruelty of life.

As you will probably surmise with little help from me, a 12-year-old boy doesn't often pack on the pounds by living an overly active lifestyle. When I was twelve, exercise in general was excruciatingly painful (to even think about, really). Dragging my ass up a mountain was at the top of my list for most barbaric and most torturing of all activities.

You see, fit people don't exactly understand what it's like to be fat and hike. The way it always worked was this. The troop and the leaders would hike, hike, hike, merry and happy as ever. "Oh look at that beautiful bird," I'd hear them say in the far off distance. "Let's pick up the pace," I'd hear someone else say. With time, I would lag behind by two to thirty switchbacks. Dying. Wanting to die.

Every so often, someone would look back and say, "where's Danny?" There would be grumbles and everyone would sit down to rest and eat granola bars while I caught up. Eventually I would round a bend and make eye contact with the group. There they all were, sitting on boulders and logs, drinking from their canteens, laughing, waiting. It was always so disconcerting to walk up to their loud sighs, their groans, and their rolling eyes. I was doing my best not to die. Couldn't they see that?

As soon as I reached the pack, everyone would immediately stand up. Our leader would say, "okay, let's move," and away they'd go. I'd pause for a moment, desperate for a break. Desperate to sit down. Desperate to get a drink. Desperate to do anything but take another step. But I never got to because that would put me behind even further which would be the same thing as admitting that I was *really* fat.

One particular afternoon, my troop was hiking to Horsetail Falls. The trail to get there is wide and easy to follow, though it's steep and a couple of hours by the time you hit the falls.

That particular year also brought out the Bitchin' clothing brand. All the cool kids wore Bitchin' shorts that basically looked like cut-off MC Hammer pants with drawstring waistbands. I always tied mine in a double-knot since yanking each other's shorts down was also trending. And, as I did *every* day back then, I was wearing those Bitchin' shorts on the hike. Or at least I was wearing them for most of it.

About half way up, my troop got so far ahead of me that I could no longer see or hear anyone. I was wheezing and gasping along, stepping over exposed roots and rocks when the feeling hit me. *Oh crap. Oh crap. Oh crap. Oh crap.* I suddenly had to poop, and I had to poop *bad*.

Without a single other thought, I speed-waddled off the trail and disappeared to find a place to do my business. Time was against me. I began yanking at my drawstring. My double knot had cinched so tight that there was no undoing it. I crossed my legs and clenched my ever-pressurizing bum as tightly as I could while I continued working on it. I still couldn't get it. I had seconds left. I still couldn't get it.

My eyes bulged, my mouth clenched, and I freaking *lost* it. I pooped my pants. And it wasn't just poop. It was more like runny baby food as evidenced by both the feel and sound of it.

I assure you, the last thing any twelve-year old wants to do is shit his pants while he's out with the kids who will make or break his entire social existence for the next six years.

So, I did what any kid in my situation would do, and I freaked the hell out. I panicked.

I stood there with pants full of diarrhea and the thought of every *wrong* thing to do began flooding into my young mind.

I could live in the woods. That was an option. I could walk around the long side of the mountains and sneak home. That would only be about 16 miles or so. I could walk around until I found a cougar or a bear and offer myself up as a succulent and fatty sacrifice. Believe me. Any of those options were better than the alternative of anyone *ever* finding out what had just transpired in my Bitchin' shorts.

Then, at the very peak of my agonizing horror, I heard it off in the distance. Raging water. A river. Yes, that was my ticket out of this mess (pun intended). I could just make my way to the river, wash my shorts out, and return back to the group after they dried. My plan was fool proof. It would be easy. It was genius.

After considerable additional effort, I finally worked open the draw string, removed my boots, and carefully stepped out of my now heavy underwear.

The accident had left my skivvies unfixable, so I tossed them under a nearby tree. At the very least they would be a deterrent for poop-fearing predators who certainly would smell it from miles away and keep their distance. My shorts, they could be washed. They were bad, but not *too* bad. And so, with my Bitchins' clenched in hand, I put my boots back on and started walking toward the sound of the water... Naked from the waist down, just as I had been when the good doctor publicly studied my junk just weeks earlier.

But, no matter how far I walked, the sound of the river *never* seemed to get closer. Sticks, branches, and shrubs continually assaulted my naked legs. I must have walked for more than an hour before I finally reached it. And "it" wasn't the river. "It" was a 100 foot nearly vertical ravine towering above the river, impossible to descend. *What to do, what to do...* I looked around desperately. I looked toward the water below.

There was no way I could get down that thing in one piece. And there was sure as hell no way I would ever get back up it.

So, not wanting only poopy naked pieces of me to be found by hunters months or maybe even years later, I thought back and remembered a tiny two-inch trickle of water that we had crossed on the trail at one point. That was my only option. Still half naked, I made my way back through the woods. Back toward the trail. It took another hour or so to get back.

I finally found the trail. My legs were purple and bleeding. My inner thighs were covered in excruciating rashes. My walk was becoming increasingly bow-legged as I went.

I looked up the trail. The troop was probably at the falls by now, having a good time, enjoying themselves. I knew I'd better hurry if I was to run into them on the way down with clean, *dry* shorts.

I made my way down the trail, found the trickle of water, sat down in the middle of it and began washing my nethers as best I could, praying like Moses that nobody came from either direction while I was sitting there. I cleaned the shorts as much as they could be cleaned. I got rid of any evidence of the event, wrung out my Bitchins', and snuck back off into the woods while I waited for them to dry.

As it turned out, it takes a while to go from soaking wet to dry without a trace of foul play. The sun was starting to go down when they were finally dry enough to venture out. I put them on and again painfully made my way back to the trail. No sign of the group. I figured they were still above me making their way down. I headed down the first mile alone, not wanting them to have to wait for me when they did catch up. That would just be more embarrassing, and I was sure that the more time we spent together, the higher the chance that they'd figured out what had transpired in my undies.

I came up with a story I would tell. I just got lost. I took a wrong trail. I never could find them again, so I just headed back down. Yeah, it was believable. Nobody would ever know the truth.

The sun had disappeared by the time I neared the bottom of the trail. Only trace amounts of twilight made it possible to see where I was walking. Within minutes the sky would be black. I kept wondering why my comrades hadn't caught up to me yet.

I emerged at the bottom of the trail to a *sea* of familiar faces. A couple dozen or so adults were hovered around the hoods of SUVs, looking at maps. Car after car was parked at the bottom of the trail, and more were arriving.

It was the beginning of a search party. They were forming a *fucking* search party. For me.

My entire troop was standing at the bottom. My leader noticed me and sprinted over with the happiest, most annoyed, most horrified look I had ever seen. "Where have you been?" His eyes were glossed with panic. The kind of panic that says, "Holy Crap Batman. I lost someone else's kid in the woods."

"I got lost."

"What do you mean you got lost?"

"I accidentally took another trail when it forked." Others were crowding around me. I was thankful for the blackness that obscured the scrapes, rashes, and bruises.

My leader shook his head. "There are no other trails. And this trail is like six feet wide. How could you get lost?"

"I don't know, I just did!" I was desperate for them not to keep digging. Without another word, I broke free from the questioning crowd and headed toward my father's vehicle that had just pulled up. He asked me the same questions, I gave him the same answers, and I stuck to my story. No matter how many people grilled me about it over the weeks which followed, or how many people insisted that getting lost on that trail was impossible, I never wavered on my story. Ever.

And I learned a valuable lesson that day. I learned that when my abilities are limited, I need to man up and admit those limitations to the group. I learned that it's okay to ask for what I need when others are more advanced, abler, or more educated than I.

Other people can't always read my mind, and they will never be able to understand *my* limitations when *they* don't experience those same limitations. This hike to all of them was an easy hike. They never became so winded that they feared that their hearts would quit working. They only thought my legs moved slower because I was fat. They didn't understand that my heart was also pumping so much faster because I never communicated that to them. Instead, I tried to hide it, which just made things worse for me.

I also learned that when I do something embarrassing that might affect others, I just need to man up and admit that, too. There have been very few times when my cover-ups didn't lead to more embarrassment for me or bigger problems for others.

I have found that this world is generally very forgiving of embarrassing mistakes or weaknesses, *when* the perpetrator confesses it and owns it. I've also found that when the perpetrator works to cover it up and lies about it, the world generally becomes obsessed with uncovering the truth and bringing about confession and justice.

But of all the lessons I learned the day they formed a search party for the Boy Scout who crapped his pants, I learned that I need to never, ever, *ever* again tie my Bitchin' shorts into place with a double knot.

The Unfortunate Nipple Incident

I once got my nipple ripped off. Er, mostly anyway.

It was that same summer I crapped my pants.

I think it's safe to say that the universe had a big helping of humility that it was sadistically enjoying spoon feeding to me one giant bite at a time.

I was at that Boy Scout summer camp with my troop for the week. A lot of shenanigans go on at those camps. Some kids even *die*.

Okay, I said that just to be dramatic.

Anyway, down in the pond there were all sorts of old, colorful, rusted canoes. One day, several troops challenged ours to a canoe sinking war. And believe me, when you're twelve, nobody is going to turn that action down. So, I climbed into a canoe with a couple other guys, and we all paddled to the middle of the treacherous (four-foot-deep) pond and waited for the whistle to blow. Yes, this was an approved, event. There must have been fifteen or twenty canoes, all with two or three Boy Scouts in each one.

Let me explain to you how canoe sinking wars work, and then we shall all sit back together and question why any adult in their right mind would sanction such a brutal and potentially injury-inducing activity.

There are no rules. Not really. You just do everything you can to tip and sink the other guys' canoes. The last one floating is the big winner. I think they were awarded a beaver pelt or some other odd thing. The Scouting program is weird like that.

So, when that whistle did blow, you can just imagine the mayhem and craziness of it all. I still have Vietnam-type flashbacks from that day. Screams. Flailing arms. Splashing. Yelling. Groans. Grunts. Smashing. Thrashing. And every other crazy thing you can imagine.

Being the big tall fat kid who had hit puberty well before most of his peers had its advantages. My canoe seemed more stable than the others. I had a longer reach than the scrawny twigs coming at us from the other canoes. I had grip strength that could only come from, well, you know, *gripping* things with vigor (thus the puberty advantage). And, I was just plain old scary looking to kids that were half my size.

Canoe after canoe started going down. I roared with delight each time we sent one under. Kids everywhere were morosely dragging their canoes to shore. We actually had a shot at winning this thing.

After sinking the canoe of two weaklings who didn't stand a chance, we found ourselves parallel to a couple of equally sizable and equally scary looking fellas. They were still a good three or four feet away and hadn't noticed us as they were currently working to sink a boat full of dweebs on the other side of them.

"Move me closer guys!" I yelled to the boys on the other end of my canoe. If I could just reach… out… a little… closer…

A little closer…

"A little closer!"

And then it happened.

I was stretched out across the edge of my canoe, across that final span of water, and then I got hold of it. A firm grip on the other canoe! That mother-freaker was going down (I didn't have my mad cussing skills back then).

As I labored with all my determination to push the edge of the other canoe under the water, I don't know what happened next for sure. All I know was that my end of the canoe suddenly swung hard toward their end of their canoe, and I felt pain like I'd never felt before.

I screamed and looked down toward the source of the hurt.

The two canoes had come together and pinched my nipple hard and fast between their metal edges and they had ripped that sucker off. Er, mostly, anyway.

Small amounts of blood began flowing immediately down my chest in fantastically awful trickle patterns. My right nipple was hanging like a flap, still connected by a small amount of tissue. My eyes widened. I stopped breathing completely while my heart reconnected with my brain.

I didn't scream again after that. The pain was too incredible. I just stared at the freaky hanging flap of a nipple that now dangled like raw bacon on a fork.

Then I slid my finger under the flap and folded it back up into the bloody mess above it. When I let go, it flopped down again and instead of holding my breath this time, I started hyperventilating.

I don't remember what happened in the canoe war after that. I don't know if we won or lost. I don't remember if I attempted to keep playing or if I gave up at that point. I don't know if anyone noticed the blood flowing down. I only remember that horrid little flap surrounded by raw, red tissue. I remember my stomach knotting up as I lifted the flap. I remember my panic.

I also remember that I decided not to tell any of the leaders when it happened. Instead, I snuck into my tent, got into my first aid kit, and taped my nipple back on after the bleeding finally stopped. For the next two weeks I walked around putting pressure on it non-stop. At night I stacked books on top of it to keep the pressure in place. I was going to fix it, dang it. I wouldn't go through life without my nipple.

And, somehow it healed back in place. To this day I look back and wonder how I didn't die of an infection or why the tissue reconnected at all. I just know I still have two nipples and you can't really tell anything ever happened by looking at me. I certainly can, though. The healed nipple is overly ticklish and extremely sensitive, which <ahem> women seem to pick up on very quickly.

Anyway. Once bandaged up, I spread the story myself at first. But then, the nipple incident spread gloriously to all the camps around us and made me a bit of a Scout Camp celebrity that year.

"I heard it ripped all the way off!"

"I heard he sewed it back on himself!"

"Pearce picked his own nipple up out of the bottom of the canoe and he's got it in a Coke bottle in his tent."

I was very content letting the rumors get bigger and better. I never bothered correcting any of them.

Random boys would accost me and ask if it was true. Other boys would ask if they could see it. My friends bragged that they knew me. It was the first time ever that I was really, *really* cool.

Unfortunately, a couple weeks later, Brandon Taylor, another boy in my troop, got a fish hook in the cheek and everyone forgot all about my ripped off nipple.

For the next two months all anyone could talk about was Brandon Taylor and the fish hook in his cheek.

"An inch higher and it would have taken out his eye!"

"I heard he didn't even scream or anything. Even when the guy with the fishing pole yanked back on it thinking he'd caught a snag!"

"I heard it went all the way through his cheek and hooked into his gums!"

My time as a gruesome hero was done. I would try bringing up my nipple to shift the attention back to me, but it didn't matter. People were over it.

And I learned that popularity and attention from others will always be fleeting when they are based on a single moment in time.

No person actually becomes popular or respected because of a solitary incident. To remain a phenomenon, one has to remain phenomenal.

And since ripping off body parts or taking on new injuries every time the attention dies down isn't realistic (for most of us), that means people have to *constantly* do things and say things that will keep them fresh in the minds of others. As soon as they stop, someone, somewhere else will step in and take the limelight. This is the law of popularity.

But... Respect? That's something else altogether. A person becomes respected by standing behind his beliefs. He becomes respected as a result of his integrity, and his ongoing passion or devotion over long periods of time. These are definitely characteristics that can make a person popular, as well. The difference is, respected people are content in or out of the limelight. Popular people *always* have to find a way to be in it.

Because of that, every one of us who enjoys the limelight (and I truly believe there is nothing wrong with that) has to decide whether we want to be respected in the limelight or whether we want to be popular in the limelight.

And, I can tell you. I craved popularity once I lost my nipple fame. I didn't crave respect.

The older I get, the more I shun popularity and the more I value being respected, even if that means my time in the limelight comes and goes.

I don't want to be the man who shocked the world just to shock the world. I don't want to be the man who served others only to serve himself. I don't want to be the man who did out-of-the-ordinary things just to get people talking about him and wanting more of him.

I want to be the man who was known for saying and doing the things that he felt was right, whether those ideas and actions were popular or not. I want to be the man who served others because serving others was the right thing to do. I want to be the man who did out-of-the-ordinary things because ordinary things just weren't satisfying to him. In other words, I want to live a life that's worthy of the respect that I seek from others.

And I know that if I live my life in such a way, the frequency with which I have to be in the spotlight to remain constant in the minds of others will lessen with time until I don't have to be there at all. Those who seek popularity instead of respect will never get to experience that. They will be forgotten quickly once they withdraw. Of this I am certain.

Stuck

It's amazing what a year can do for an awkward boy. Twelve months after the canoeing incident, I was a whole new person. Literally. I'd gained about an inch in height and a good three to eleven inches on my waist. Yes, I had officially passed through the stage of chubby preteen and entered my next much more awesome stage, fat teenager.

But I was *very* cool despite that. I still rocked the jigsaw puzzles, I had a closet full of plaid flannel, and I now sported a trendy and perfect bowl-cut. The grease look was in, so I was now careful not to shower more than once every four or five days. I'm sure I smelled like a wet bear coming out of hibernation, but everyone else did, too, so nobody noticed. Except maybe our parents and the teachers at our junior high.

God bless junior high school teachers.

I've always thought that a junior high school teacher could create the world's most popular blog simply by sharing the weirdness she sees going on every day. Middle school kids have to be the most awkward, most disgusting, and most lost human beings on the planet. Nobody looks back at junior high with fondness. Nobody looks back and says, "oh, I looked *good* with my face covered in giant white heads and those rosy splotches where I went to town on other giant white heads." Nobody looks back and says, "I had *all* the right answers back then." And nobody looks back and says, "I really miss my corduroy overalls that weren't long enough to cover my socks. God, it was so sexy the way they hugged my crotch and left nothing to the imagination." I'm telling you. *Nobody* says that. Not honestly.

What I do look at fondly is all the lessons I learned in that weird transitional stage between child and adult. I really believe more life-shaping lessons are learned between the ages of 11 and 22 than the rest of life put together. And, for some reason, Scout camps were where I learned a *lot* of those lessons.

A year after the nipple incident, I found myself once again standing at attention every morning, watching a flag be raised, hand to heart. One morning someone had attached a pair of poopy underwear to the flagpole and hoisted it before we got there. It was epic. And they weren't mine, which was a big bonus.

There was a small lake outside of camp, and on the edge was a fifteen-foot tower that the Scouts would climb up one at a time. They'd grab onto a metal bar hooked to a wire, and zip line into the lake while dangling precariously. I'd done it successfully many times, but on one occasion I had wet hands and slipped as I leapt from the tower. I immediately fell fifteen feet straight down, and cut my foot open on a stick. My pride was hurt, but not as much as when my entire troop came up with a cheer for the cheer contest: *689! 689! Danny fell off the zip cord line!* We won the contest.

And who am I kidding. I acted like I was offended, but I felt like a mini celebrity once again, having my name chanted to the entire camp like that.

I also was a master marksman at the shooting range. I only got yelled at twice that year for accidentally pointing my loaded rifle at another human being.

God bless Scout leaders.

After we were done with our activities for the day, my friends and I would sneak into the shooting range and go dig all the lead bullets out of the logs behind the targets. We'd carve out shapes in wood, melt the lead in tin cans, and mold ourselves fantastic pendants and tokens.

When we were done, our hands were laced with lead, our clothes were laced with lead, and I'm pretty sure I used my teeth on several occasions to pull tiny slivers of wood out of the lead once it had hardened and cooled. How any of us had kids when we were older is beyond me.

Oh wait, my wife and I adopted because my sperm don't work quite right. I am just now putting two and two together. And all these years I thought it was because I had nuked my testis with my laptop. Could I be infertile because I constantly gnawed on bullets as a Boy Scout? *Hm.*

Anyway, back to Boy Scout camp and all the fun to be had there.

At this particular summer camp, there were no bathrooms or even outhouses. Our leaders had chosen to take us somewhere a little more raw than usual. And, as it did three to five times a day for a boy with irritable bowel syndrome, nature called and demanded a place further away than the nearest tree trunk.

I began walking deep into the woods looking for the perfect spot, far away from the camp. Everyone knew that dropping a twosie where anyone ever saw it or smelled it led to immediate ridicule and chastisement from the group. And so I walked. And walked. And walked. I really didn't want to squat for this one. My last trip into the woods had ended with burning quads and a poop smear down the back of my shorts because my chubby legs wouldn't bend far enough, for long enough. And so, I walked, searching for a place I could sit down to make this happen.

And then I saw it. A tall pine tree had uprooted and tipped over not too long before. The pine needles were still green. There was one area halfway up the tree where the branches had been stripped away and the trunk had split in two. The way it sat left a five-inch gap between the two halves. It was the perfect nature-made toilet.

All the walking had been so worth it. This would be my secret little spot for the rest of the week.

I pulled my pants to my ankles, centered myself over the hole, and sat down on the log. *I'm a genius*, I thought. No strain. No work. No incriminating evidence on the back of my pants. Plenty of broad leafed plants were within arm's reach for the cleanup side of things.

In no hurry to get back and help with dinner, I stayed on that log for a good twenty minutes. It was so peaceful. Chipmunks were chirping at each other in the distance. A woodpecker was searching for a meal nearby. A cool mountain breeze mingled with the hot summer sun and danced across my face to nature's background symphony.

Finally, I grabbed a few leaves, wadded them up, and leaned forward. Except, I *couldn't* lean forward. My skin had somehow *attached* itself to the log.

I pulled a little harder. It didn't give.

I pulled even harder. Still I was stuck. And I'd be lying if I said I wasn't starting to panic.

I took a deep breath and really studied that log for the first time since I had arrived at my genius getaway commode. Oozing through the cracks was thick, sticky sap. I poked at some of it with my finger and a glob fastened to it. I pulled it away and squished it with my thumb. Immediately, as if by super glue, my digits stuck together. After considerable effort, I pulled them apart again which was when I realized the real predicament I was in.

My bare ass was glued to a log in the middle of the woods.

I spent the next ten minutes or so willing the bond to give. I don't think I ever prayed as hard for a miracle as I did during that ten minutes, either. And then, in the distance behind me, someone shouted my name.

Oh, crap, I thought.

I knew what had to be done. I certainly wasn't going to be sitting there like a dunce with my pants around my ankles while they came searching for me. I could just see a crowd of boys and leaders standing around me, scratching their heads trying to figure out what to do. *How the heck do we pry this fat kid off of this log?*

Whoever it was in the distance called my name again.

It's like tearing off a Band-Aid, I remember telling myself. I closed my eyes, counted to three, and forcefully tried to stand up.

Still I was stuck. This was going to be a lot worse than a Band-Aid.

Again, I heard my name. This time by someone else. "I'm coming!" I screamed in panic, willing the voices to stay far, far away.

I closed my eyes one more time and *ripped* myself off of the log.

I will not spend multiple paragraphs trying to explain my pain in that moment. I will only tell you that once free, I looked down and there were tiny bits of my flesh stuck to that tree.

Again, someone called my name. I yanked my pants up and ran toward camp. I never did wipe my butt.

Later that night, I went into my tent and pulled out a fresh pair of white Fruit of the Looms (something I had plenty of since I brought a new pair for every day and hadn't changed them even once). I pulled off the pair I had hurriedly pulled up in the woods, and grimaced as my wounds detached from the cloth. I pulled on the new pair and held up the old ones. Several dark reddish-black blood spots had formed and dried. A brown smear had streaked its way up the middle of them.

The next morning, I walked into the woods again and buried the underwear beneath a pile of old pine needles.

Looking back, I really wish I would have kept that pair of undies. I was taught a big lesson that day, and I should have looked at that underwear as a trophy. They really should have been framed and hung on display where I could see them every day.

It was from that experience, after all, that I learned we all will have genius ideas from time to time, and I also learned that sometimes those genius ideas end up being really stupid. They fail. They don't work. And sometimes they even hurt us or set us back. But we can't ever *know* that until we follow through on those ideas and see where they take us.

At the same time, I also have learned over my life that sometimes our genius ideas really do end up being just that. Genius. They *don't* fail, and amazing things happen. Likewise, we can't ever know *that* until we follow through on those ideas and see where they take us as well.

If we decide that we're okay always having a little poop on the back of our shorts, we will never actually find the solution that will fix it. If we're afraid of getting stuck to a log in the woods, we'll never find the *right* place to sit down next time.

We will win some and lose some, but the more we see where our genius and creative thoughts take us, the less we'll lose and the more we'll win as we get better and better at knowing which ideas are sound, and which aren't.

At least that's what me and a bloody pair of underwear like to think.

The Broken Wrist

There was this weird period between getting super-glued to that log at Scout camp and burning down my parents' basement some three years later. It's all one big blur.

I'd like to think I can't remember much from that time span because I had my nose buried in my books or because I was off being *awesome* somewhere, but I'm pretty sure I don't remember it because I spent most of it either yanking my crank or playing Nintendo at my friend's house.

Here is what I do remember of those three years.

Chocolate milk and a half dozen donuts were a great daily snack to eat while conquering Zelda or Mario Bros. Eyeglasses that would tint in the sun became popular. For about two weeks. Which is right when I got my pair that I'd have to wear for the next two years at least. Hell's existence was proven to me by walking through it every day in the halls of my junior high school. Finding shoes in a size 13 wasn't easy. Finding hats made for gorilla-sized heads proved even more difficult. It was impossible to get to my next class on time when my gym coach insisted that the fat kids actually *finish* the mandatory "Fun Run" every Thursday. I had magical powers that made all but the odorous parts of me invisible to girls.

And, I broke my wrist.

Again, I'd like to say that I was doing something glorious and *awesome* when I broke it. I'd like to tell you I was playing football, or street fighting, or beating up some jerk with impossible biceps at school, but I wasn't. I was walking down a sidewalk, probably on my way to buy my daily maple bars, when I tripped on a heightened slab of concrete and landed square on my wrists, fracturing one of them.

The moment I landed, I *knew* I had broken it. You only have to break a bone once to know what it feels like, and I had broken several before that moment. In fact, my entire existence started with a broken collar bone. Apparently almost 10 lb. babies aren't made to go through such tiny silly things as birth canals and pelvic bones, but out I finally was pushed, and snap went my collar bone on the way.

After I broke my wrist that day, some 13 years later, I sat on the ground making that awful sound people make when they're hurt but they want to be tougher than the pain. It sounds a lot like a gross and inexperienced person getting lucky with their very unlucky partner, except my grunts and groans lasted much longer, I'm sure. "Ooooh, ooh, aah, eeeee, ooooh, aaah, rrrrr, grrr, ooooh, aaahaaahah. Rrrrr." You know, like that. You've done it too. Guaranteed.

I finally picked myself up and carried my limp wrist in to Mom, and told her I was pretty sure I had broken it.

"Nah, it's just a sprain," she said as she wiggled it back and forth and up and down. I winced in pain as she did so.

I insisted that it felt like it was broken.

Again she insisted that it wasn't. It couldn't be.

And, since I was a teenager with no transportation and no way to get medical care on my own, I finally said "okay" and was just really careful with it for the next few days.

As it happened, I had an appointment to have my tonsils removed three days later.

We were escorted to a hospital room where I was told to get naked and put on a gown. Mom left the room so I could change. I stripped down to the buff, pulled the gown on, and looked down. It was so short that my nethers were flapping in the breeze below. I mention this for no reason except to point out how ridiculously tall I was for a teenager of that age. Or maybe I mention it to make you believe (without having to tell some big lie) that I was *very* well endowed. After all, you may have been picturing a gown that went to my knees, and who am I to stop your assumptions?

Anyway, since having your mom see your dangling nethers isn't the most fun thing, I hurried and got under the hospital blanket and waited for them to come back into the room.

Mom returned and kept me company. Eventually a nurse followed with a clipboard in tow. First she listened to my heart. Then she took my blood pressure. Then she checked my pulse.

Back then, they didn't use fancy gadgets that clip onto the end of your fingertips. They grabbed your wrist and manually counted the beats.

And, as you'll remember, my wrist was *broken*.

The nurse grabbed my wrist and pulled it off the bed. Immediately I jerked away and yelped in anguish. If you've ever had a broken bone, you know the pain that comes from moving it or putting pressure on it the wrong way.

The nurse looked at me and said, "*what* was *that*? Is there something wrong with your wrist?"

In that moment, I didn't answer, but looked over at Mom instead. She sat suddenly so rigid in her chair. Her arms were stiff. Her eyebrows were raised. The blood rushed out of her. And I saw it in her eyes. She knew that she'd made a *really* bad judgment call and she was feeling like the mother failure of the decade.

I smugly looked at the nurse again and said, "yeah I think I broke it. My mom thinks it's just sprained and she wouldn't take me to the doctor." In that moment, I wanted to punish her with shame and embarrassment and remind her that sometimes I could be right about things, too.

The nurse assured us both that it's not normal for a person to grimace and jerk away in pain like that. Not when it's just a sprain. "Don't worry, we'll take care of that," she said. Not too much later they injected me with something dreamlike and amazing, and I danced with the heaviness of it as the blackness settled in and put me to sleep.

I awoke with a blood-filled stomach, the worst sore throat of my life, and a cast on my arm. I felt nauseated. Sitting by my side was Mom. I had never seen her look so concerned about anything before. She had seven kids at that point; empathy and compassion often had to take a backseat to taking care of the rest of life.

Suddenly I threw up an impossible amount of blood into a bowl that was quickly shoved under my schnoz. It made me feel instantly better. Mom removed the blood-filled dish and I leaned back in the bed again.

"They did an X-Ray while you were out, and you were right. Your arm was broken," she said. Then she found no fewer than ten different ways between five different blood-pukes to apologize to me for letting me go three days with a broken arm. She really was sorry.

I just thought it was cool that I had a cast that my friends could sign. I had already punished her before the surgery with my smug statement to the nurse.

I held my casted arm up in the air, looked at it, and told her it was okay.

I learned something from that experience. I learned that there will be times in my life when other people make mistakes that affect me personally and may even cause me undue or prolonged pain.

And, I can either hold it above them when they do, or I can find a way to laugh about it and forgive them for their errors.

It's such a platitude, but it's *so* true: we live in an imperfect world. The everyday people who surround you and me are far more imperfect than any of us would like to think or admit. And since you and I are some of those everyday people, it means that we are just as imperfect as well.

You and I are going to make mistakes just like Mom made sometimes. Every one of us will make them.

You and I are going to do things that hurt the people we love, even though we don't mean to. Sometimes we will even mean to hurt them.

We're going to do things we wish we could take back. We're going to do things we feel make us failures. We're going to do things that will make us question our very goodness and intelligence and morality. We are going to do crappy things that we fear will have some power to define us forever more.

And when we do, don't we *all* hope that others will find a way to laugh about it and forgive it? Once the dust settles, and the cast is set, at least?

I could have held that mistake above my mother indefinitely. I could have brought it up every time she thought I was wrong. I could have brought it up every time I thought she needed a lesson from me in parental humility. I could have brought it up for the rest of her life. I saw it in her eyes. It was something she felt so badly about that I could have held it above her and used it against her.

But what good would that have done? I knew it was an accident. I knew she didn't do it on purpose. I knew it wasn't indicative of her true character.

Oh sure, I bring it up with her as a humorous jab here and there. But I love my mother, so I'm not going to do anything more than that. Not when I want the same courtesy from others. Not when I want the same courtesy from her for all the mistakes I made and will *always* continue to make.

Burning Down the Basement
Well, Almost

Shortly after my sister Tomi Ann's 16th birthday, she got all prettied up and headed out the door with some floppy-haired weirdo for her first date. I watched her zip in and out of the different rooms of our house as she got ready for her big debut into the world of love. She was on cloud nine for sure, and if I remember right, her feet didn't touch the floor once during the last hour. I found it annoying. And magical. Okay, I'll be honest. I was jealous.

The rest of the family was so excited for her, especially Mom and Dad. She was the oldest kid and it was the first time *any* of their kids had gone out on a date. You see, in strict Mormon families, your parents don't let you date until you're at least sixteen.

But she wasn't the only one who would bring excitement to the family that night. An hour or two after she left, all hell would break loose.

I had done something bad. I have no idea what it was. I probably went to a friend's house when I was supposed to be doing homework. Or I didn't do my chores. Or maybe I just begged one too many times to be allowed to date as well.

My punishment for whatever bad thing I did was to go down to the basement and clean the kitchen and family room while the rest of the family watched a movie and ate popcorn upstairs.

Holy shit. I just realized that was very Cinderella-like. I probably didn't even do anything bad. I probably was this sweet blonde-haired boy who only had mice for friends, and I was down there working because I was *too* awesome for them to be nice to.

No, I definitely did something bad. I was kind of mean to my family, usually rebellious, always argumentative, and in general, I was eternally just a big butt to all of them. At least as a teenager.

Anyway, after arguing (I'm sure) about my punishment, I huffed and puffed down the stairs and begrudgingly got to work.

There were boxes stacked all over the place. Mom had been canning jams and peaches for days as she worked on another favorite Mormon past time, getting the family's one-year food storage in place. As part of my cleaning punishment, it was my job to take all the boxes of jars and stack them up against the back wall of the storage room where they would probably get dusty and grimy over the next years as we held off eating them should disaster or calamity suddenly strike.

Now, before I go any further, let me tell you that I *know* this is only the 11th chapter in this book and I've already centered two of them around pooping. Get over it. I pooped a lot as a kid. And frankly, I think you're weird if you didn't.

And, this one also involved pooping, though, lucky you, the pooping was just a side note.

Now, back to poor CinderDanny, slaving away in the basement while his family lived it up without him.

I had about half of the boxes put away and had just picked up another one when my bowels demanded immediate attention. Yep, I had to poop. Again, get over it.

I set the box down on top of the stove in the basement kitchen and went to do my business while I got lost in an issue of Sports Illustrated. Swimsuit Edition.

What I didn't notice was my ever-enlarging gut bumping the burner control-knob when I set the box down, turning the stove on high.

A couple minutes later, still planted firmly on the John, staring at the mostly exposed breasts of one fabulous Tyra Banks, the smoke alarm in the hall outside the bathroom went off.

Other smoke alarms started sounding about the same time that I heard Dad's booming voice yell out to me and ask where I was.

Then the ever-so-powerful smell of smoke began seeping through the cracks of the bathroom door.

Dad started hollering that the basement was on fire, and everyone should immediately get out of the house.

Not knowing I had anything to do with it, I jumped to attention and took care of the important things before exiting the bathroom. I wiped my ass. And I stashed the Sport's Illustrated, hoping beyond hope that it would survive whatever inferno was on the other side of that bathroom door. Once the contraband was well-hidden, I walked out of the bathroom and into straight-up mayhem.

The top foot or two of the basement hallway was filled with smoke. I could see smoke pushing its way up the stairwell and into the story above. I ran to the place from which the smoke was pouring and saw that the box of jams I had set on the stove was ablaze with huge flames. The wall behind the stove had caught fire as well, and just as I yelled to see if anyone else was down there, Dad and Mom both came barreling down the stairs and past me toward the flames.

Mom was carrying a fire extinguisher. Dad yelled at me to go join the other kids in the front yard. I immediately did as I was told.

I would learn later that Mom had sprayed the fire with the extinguisher several times, and on each attempt, would receive a jolt of electricity. Don't ask me what that was all about. I don't deeply understand sciency-things like that.

I exited the house and found my five younger siblings all standing out in the winter cold in their pajamas and coats. A few inches of snow covered the grass to either side of them. I stood next to them and we all looked at the house which now had our two parents inside as smoke starting to pour from the upper levels.

Within a couple minutes, Mom and Dad emerged and joined us, unable to put out the fire. At that exact moment, our neighbor Tim Porter arrived. He was a firefighter. Mom and Dad quickly told him what was going on. They had gotten some of the fire out, but there were still flames since the jams just wouldn't extinguish. They followed him into the house and down into the basement where he used his big fireman gloves to pat the fire out before it could spread again.

Our next door neighbor had appeared next to us kids at some point, and when we saw windows starting to open in the upper levels, she knew it was safe for everyone inside, and she took my brother and sisters over to her house to wait somewhere far less icy and scary. I refused her invitation, and stayed planted right where I was.

Scared. And horrified.

I had just caught my family's home on fire. I didn't know what had happened, but I knew that it was my fault. I knew it had to do with that box of jars I had set on the stovetop. I knew I had almost killed my family. I knew I had almost burned down the entire house. And I knew I was going to be in more trouble than I had ever been in before.

After every window and door had been opened, Mom and Dad walked out, followed by Tim Porter. I slowly closed my eyes as I waited for the shit storm to start hailing down.

But it never did.

Dad walked over, put his arm around me, and asked if I was okay. I just nodded.

Mom walked over and linked arms with me and told me it was all okay. They got it put out before much damage happened at all.

Tim Porter stood several feet away just looking at the house, deciding if any more action was needed on his part.

Then we all just stood in silence until the emergency vehicles began arriving.

Tomi Ann arrived home from her first date to fire trucks and police cars outside her home. The look on her face as she exited the car was unforgettable and priceless.

When it was over, we all went to sleep at my aunt's house, and I lay awake most of the night. I could have killed my parents. I could have killed my siblings. The entire house could have burned down. We could have lost everything. My Sports Illustrated might have been gone forever. How did it happen? Why did it happen?

Mom and Dad must have been in shock. I was sure that I had it coming to me the next day. There was no way I would escape much-deserved wrath on this one.

But their wrath never did come. Not the next day, or the day after that. In fact, not ever.

Instead, Mom and Dad both laughed about it. They laughed about the fire. They laughed about Mom getting zapped with electricity over and over. They laughed about the burnt walls and cabinets. They laughed about the jams that just *wouldn't* go out. They laughed about the melted kitchen faucet. They laughed about the smoky smell in the house. They laughed about it all. And never once did they point blame at me or get angry with me.

I tried to apologize. They just laughed it off every time I did, and told me not to worry about it.

I would just look at them in disbelief. These were the people who got mad at me for scraping my fork on my plate or for leaving the front door open. They were the strictest and sternest parents I knew of at the time. And yet, they were laughing after I had made the biggest mistake of my life.

The lessons that resulted from the fire and the aftermath were many, and also shaped much of my parenting today.

I learned that a good parent *knows* when the natural consequences of a bad action are punishment enough for their child. They know when their child is suffering because of bad choices, and they don't rub his nose in it or make him suffer further.

I have no doubt that my parents could see the remorse in my eyes the same way I could see it in Mom's eyes when she realized my wrist was actually broken. And when they saw it, they did what good parents do best. They laughed. They forgave. And they forgot.

More or less.

Just like with the broken wrist, they still find ways to humorously bring it up in jabbing ways. We like to laugh together about it to this day. We reminisce back to the look on Tomi Ann's face when she arrived home from her date with the floppy-haired weirdo.

Now that I'm a parent, I understand their reaction in ways that I never did before. I often think back to that fire and the way my folks handled it. And I watch for that look of remorse in Noah's eyes. The look that says, *I really need you to not punish me more right now, Dad.*

And I hope that I am always the kind of parent who knows when the punishment my child is giving himself is plenty punishment enough.

A Pointless List of
My Random Thoughts

And now, the first half of an overly pointless catalogue full of my random thoughts.

Ever since my kid has been big enough to tie quintuple-knots in my shoelaces, I've kept a list of my casual observations of life and the people in it.

- People at gas pumps groan and moan at the current price no matter what the current cost of gas is. I've come to believe that people just don't like paying for gas.
- Some people are anti-hunting, anti-killing, vegetarian animal lovers. Until they see a spider. Then, it's kill, kill, kill, at any cost.
- If you're a single dad and you want to feel like a celebrity, go join the group of moms standing outside of your kid's school, waiting for class to let out. Make them giggle, they'll make you brownies; you know, for being "such a superhero dad" and all. Beware of roofies.
- If you're a single mom and you want to feel like a celebrity, learn to want something else instead. You'll be happier. Being a superhero mom is apparently just part of your job description. It's a double standard that sucks for you, I know. Also, beware of roofies.

- There is a percentage of the population who adamantly claims they hate seafood, yet have always refused to so much as even *attempt* to taste it.
- Walmart greeters are often happy to have a job at all.
- Costco greeters seem often annoyed that they got stuck on front door duty for the day.
- There is a group of parents on the Internet whose sole purpose is to make every other parent feel as worthless as possible. These people use guilt and shame and pressure to make the rest of us feel like *everything* we do as parents is wrong, dangerous, or is causing long-term damage to our kids. These people should not be allowed on the Internet. They also should not be allowed to have kids. Or to enjoy the activities that lead to children existing.
- Clowns are perhaps the greatest irony in existence. They were invented to make the masses laugh. Now they just creep the shit out of everyone.
- All over this country, parents will happily let their young offspring attend gambling halls designed with no purpose other than to entice children to gamble away their parents' money. We know these kid-casinos as "fun centers."
- People with Android phones think they're better than people with Apple phones. People with Apple phones think they're better than everybody.
- Men care more about the size of their penises than women do and for a reason. Some guys have *monster* schlongs and we know it.
- People who work at fast food restaurants do not always wash their hands after they use the toilet. Not even after they drop a twosie. This is disgusting. I have witnessed it multiple times. Then again, I'm there eating fast food, so maybe I don't actually care so much what grossness I let enter my body.

- No matter where you sit in a movie theater, somehow it always ends up being right behind that guy who loves to listen to himself loudly critique every preview that is shown.

- Car salesmen are the nicest people on earth. You'll want them to be a part of your family. Until the moment they think you're not going to buy, then they turn into giant soggy weenies. Do not let car salesmen date your daughters. Ever.

- No matter what you choose to post on Facebook, it will always offend *someone*. This includes but is not limited to images of cats, videos of your kid taking his first steps, the phrase "I sure do love my grandma," and hyperbolic declarations of abortion, breast feeding, or legalized assault weapons.

- Some friends always let you happily pick up the check and *never* return the favor. You should not buy dinner for these types of friends.

- Crazy soccer dads are scary as hell, and it is okay to pick-up a juice box and fortuitously throw it at the back of their heads when they get too out of control, yelling at their own four-year-old for not gettin' in there and kickin' the fuckin' ball already.

- Really skinny women are often hungry and angry. I have learned that this is a well-known medical condition called *being hangry*.

- Bloggers who write and try and make money from it are usually a lot, but always at least a little, self-absorbed and narcissistic. Present company definitely included. It takes a certain amount of vanity to believe that the whole world might want to tune into your thoughts and enjoy your life alongside you.

- These bloggers will also attempt to claim that they're not like that at all and that others are. This is part of the narcissistic act. Present company definitely included.

- When you go to the dentist, suddenly anything and everything going on in your mouth is an extreme emergency that must to be taken care of *right now* before all of your teeth fall out and you end up having to pay tens of thousands of dollars to fix the damage caused by not fixing everything all at once. Here is my rule of thumb for this. If your dentist tells you that you have 14 cavities and that they're all an emergency, tell him to only fix the biggest two. You should be fine.

- While at the gym, people will fart with wild abandon during group classes, so long as there is loud music playing. They do not care how hard it hits the nostrils, whose eyes they might make water, or what sexy and toned human might be in their immediate proximity. And because there are so many people moving and sweating, they know that the chances of getting busted are slim to none, so why should they care? Relief without consequences. Can you blame anyone?

- When in much quieter yoga-type classes, people will let themselves keel over dead before they let even a single bum whisper escape their cheeks.

- There are companies that love and cherish their employees. They make life better for them. They do what they can to give them the best lives possible. On the opposite end of that spectrum is Hot Dog on a Stick. If you've seen their uniforms, you *know* what I'm talking about. Poor little teenage corn dog dippers.

- No matter how much money people make, it's never enough. This is true for the rich and poor alike. The only people who seem to be perfectly happy and content with how much they make and who never want more are, *ummm*, *hmmm*, nope. Nobody.

- As people age, there are two overwhelming complaints which will only escalate into old age: bodily ailments, and random hair growing out of random places where it has never existed before and where it should not ever exist on any person. The middle of their foreheads, the shafts of their penises, or the tops of their ears are a few such examples. I will claim up to three and no fewer than none of those.

- Pink eye is by far the most annoying infection on the planet. Anytime someone in America gets it, they are required to go visit a doctor to acquire a prescription for the drops that will treat it. Why?! We all know what pink eye is. We all know what it looks like. When I wake up with my eyes glued shut, I'd rather not waste an entire co-pay and half of my day just to watch a doctor take one glance at me, nod her head, and scribble something on a pad of paper. Four words... Over. The. Counter. Already.

- Pretty much everyone enjoys feeling superior about *something*. Except me. I'm kind of superior that way.

The Best Damn Tuba Player

At the end of sixth grade, my parents gave me a choice as I registered for my upcoming junior high classes. I could take band, orchestra, or choir. There was no option for none of the above. There was no option for anything that wouldn't ruin my social life. And there was no option for "what if I don't wanna."

But who am I kidding. Playing a musical instrument sounded like a blast. The trumpet. The trombone. The drums. They all made splendid options. There was no doubt that I was going to pick being in the band out of those three choices. I had no idea that where we then lived, band was a very serious nerd cult, and once sucked in, few people ever got out.

I added band to my roster and anxiously waited for orientation day to arrive when I would learn about all the different instruments and pick the one I would play for the next six years.

That glorious day came. I put on my best crotch-hugging corduroy coveralls, slicked my hair to one side, and entered that band room with my head held high.

Mr. Harrison, the junior high band teacher and most famed middle school music instructor in the state, instantly came to greet us when we walked in. He looked me up and down, taking in my size and physique. "What do you think you'd want to play?" he asked. His thick mustache and slanted eyes instructed me that this was a serious matter and to choose my next words wisely.

I looked around the room. I really wanted to play drums. "Drums would be fun," I said.

He gave it exactly *no* thought. "No. Too many kids want to be on percussion. What else sounds good?"

Oh.

I looked around the room, disappointed that my first choice had been shot down so quickly. "I've always loved the trumpet," I said. *Yes. That would be fun.*

Mr. Harrison squinted his eyes even closer together. "You know, Danny, your lips are probably too big to play the trumpet. I'm a trumpet player. It's a good instrument. But do you know what might really suit you?"

Oh. I prayed for him to say the trombone. "What?"

"The tuba."

Oh gosh, no.

"Ummm…"

He then spent twenty minutes convincing me that because of the size of my enormous mouth, and because of my incredible large stature, and since it would be good for my future, I should choose that big ass brass thing and commit to it for the next half-decade plus.

This is what he didn't tell me:

Only the most rotund kids are heavily recruited to play tuba. Tuba players have to lug around huge tuba cases anytime the band goes anywhere. Tubas are easy to dent and damage which will cost Mom and Dad and eventually me all sorts of money for repairs. Playing the tuba was the quickest ticket to being the nerd *within* the nerd class. Playing the tuba was something I would never want anyone else in the school to know about. And, playing the tuba was the *most* boring way to spend an hour every day. Believe me, at the junior high level, there are *no* awesome tuba parts. Unless holding the same note for 25 measures is awesome. Hint: it's not.

And because he was so adamant about it, and because Mom was sold on why it would be so good, and because I really didn't seem to have another choice at that point, I agreed to become a tubist. As we walked away that day, being in the band suddenly wasn't as exciting as it had been when I first entered that room with my head held so high.

And, starting the first day of junior high, I became a tuba playing band fag.

Band fag was the name students outside of band so blatantly placed on all of us band members. Being that I had started struggling a bit with same sex attraction about the same time that I started school that year, I never did quite latch onto the term as a term I should be proud of like so many of the other band fags did.

People inside the band took it as a compliment. They called themselves band fags and they wore the label with pride.

I suppose they could. I mean, none of them were playing the fat kid instrument. They were all banging mallets on bass drums or squawking out melodies on saxophones. They were cool, even though they were a bunch of nerds. I was just the tuba player. And everyone knew I only played it because I was fat.

Over the next few years, I would grow to really loathe playing the tuba. I would begin to blame the tuba for all of my social problems. When another kid would hit my lunch tray out of my hands, I blamed the tuba. When another kid would trip me on my way to the front of class, I blamed the tuba. When I had no real friends and my best friend left me for a group of more popular kids, I blamed the tuba.

You see, when you're junior high age, you have to blame *something*. The human mind isn't developed enough by then to realize "oh, I'm getting my ass handed to me because I have no confidence and no self-esteem," which would then allow me to work on fixing it. Instead it blames Mr. Harrison for pushing me into it, and Mom for not letting me out of it, and all the societal injustice that only lets fat kids play the tuba.

My brain was incapable of realizing nobody actually cared that I played the tuba. Instead, it became obsessed with the weird notion that *everyone* centered *every* belief about me on that damned instrument.

Come high school, Mom still wouldn't let me quit the band. I have no idea why, but I think she always believed that her mother shouldn't have let her quit so easily, and that a good parent sometimes makes her kids stick with things even if they don't want to. Especially when they're good at those things.

And, unfortunately, I was really good at the tuba. Quite unluckily, I was a complete natural at it.

Every week in both junior high and high school, I had to fill out a practice card. I was supposed to practice an hour each day. And, every week I'd fill in an hour a day but I never practiced a single minute at home that I can remember.

Mr. Harrison and later Mr. Watkins, the drill sergeant have-to-win high school band teacher, never questioned my practice cards because I was *good* at playing the tuba. I passed all of my in-class tests with flying colors. I could play anything they put in front of me. There was no reason to doubt me.

In tenth grade I had been pushed into trying Marching Band. We were good. Best in the state. 13th best in the entire country that year. And still I hated it.

During one band practice my shorts split all the way up the front *and* the back, leaving my whitie-tighties fully visible to all who dared let their eyes venture. And while the cool breeze on my nethers was pleasant, the giggles and smirks were less than ideal when I was still trying to somehow slip me and my giant tuba under the radar.

In another band practice I took a wrong step into the tuba player behind me and took us both down. Her tuba was smashed. The entire band had to stop practice to untangle us. I had to pay for a chunk of the damage out of my $5.15 per hour paycheck from Wendy's.

At the Grand Nationals Marching Band competition I came down with pneumonia. They made me march anyway. I was coughing up mucus, then puking up mucus, and I couldn't play a single note, but they couldn't have a hole on the field so they sent me out to march the show. After that, a bulldozer couldn't have pushed me onto a marching band field. Thankfully Mom and Dad didn't really care about marching band and they let me quit that so long as I stuck with regular band class.

My attempts to be allowed to switch to the baritone or trombone my sophomore year were thwarted left and right by Mr. Watkins. He'd let me switch for a week or two, but ultimately he "needed" me on the tuba, he'd end up saying.

As I entered eleventh grade, I was ready to throw my fucking tuba out the fucking window (yes, by this age I had picked up heavy cursing with my friends and was becoming quite good at it). I wanted out. I wanted to switch to choir. Or drama. Or *anything* that didn't make me the biggest underdog dud in the school. Again, I was not allowed to quit the band.

On the first day of class, Mr. Watkins told us that we had two weeks to submit an audition tape for the All State Band. It was the band that put all the best high school players in the state together for a mega-all-star-super-nerd-amazing-band-fag night full of spectacular music and talent.

I *very* half-heartedly recorded my audition tape. I hated my instrument, but I very much cared about my grades.

I introduced myself on the tape. "I'm Dan Pearce. I play the tuba" was all I said. I tried to make myself sound as boring as possible without hurting my grade or tipping off Mr. Watkins that I really didn't want to play in any extra nerdfests, no matter how high an honor it was. Then, I sat down and sight-read the music I was given without practicing it first, ran through the scales, and turned the tape in. I was sure it was just lousy enough to keep me out of the All State Band and just good enough to keep me from getting an earful about my real potential and what I *should* be *bla bla bla* from my band teacher.

Three weeks later, Mr. Watkins stood in front of the class and held up a sheet of paper. "I just received word of who will be in the All State Band this year!" he excitedly said. "And we have five students from our school who have been included!" Apparently five was a prestigious number from a single school.

"Mandy Summers will be playing fourth chair clarinet." Everyone applauded. Mandy blushed and smiled.

"Derek Smith will be playing with the percussion section." Again, applause followed. Derek fist pumped the air. Man, those drummers were so cool and no one knew it as well as they did.

Two other names were called. First chair saxophone to Michael Walberg. Fifth chair tuba to Kyle Dricks, the senior tuba player who got his knickers all twisted up anytime I accidentally was better at him in anything.

With each announcement more applause burst out, and students began holding their breath hoping that their name wouldn't be skipped. I was holding my breath praying that my name *wouldn't* be called.

"And finally, first chair tuba player to Dan Pearce. Congratulations, Dan." Again, applause rang out (from everyone except Kyle), this time mixed with sighs by those who actually wanted it. I half-heartedly smiled.

Apparently, I was the best damn tuba player in the state.

To me that just meant that I was the fattest kid and the biggest nerd there was.

And while the All State Band ended up being the *only* time I enjoyed being a band fag in the five years I played, I still couldn't walk away from the belief that the tuba was anything but social suicide.

I did, however, walk away from a nice scholarship offer that I told very few people about. I also walked away from band all-together my senior year. Once junior year ended, I didn't ask if I could quit band. I *informed* Mom and Dad and Mr. Watkins that I was quitting band. Mom and Dad didn't even argue. I think they knew that it was a fight they wouldn't win. Mr. Watkins tried. Hard. I just said no, and walked away.

Now, here I am some 17 years later, and I wonder why I think back to all of that as often as I do. I wonder what lessons had to have been learned.

And while it has taken me some time to really dissect all of it, I have learned that people have very real reasons for not wanting to be doing what you and I think they should be doing. I've learned that their reasons don't have to make sense or even be in their best interests. But it doesn't mean those reasons are invalid.

Sometimes other people's reasons include intrinsic struggles that they will never share and to which the rest of us will likely never be privy. Sometimes they are fighting battles against enemies that aren't even real, yet the battles and the enemies are both *very* real to them. And, sometimes people just don't *want* to do or don't *like* doing whatever it is we think they ought to be doing.

No matter what the "thing" is, or how good they are at it, or how good we know they can be at it, we should all learn to be more okay with other people's reasons for doing and not doing anything and the choices that result. Yes, sometimes we may give input, but ultimately we have to respect that there is not a life on Earth that belongs to us besides our own.

The tuba for me was a scapegoat for everything I was secretly feeling. I was resentful and indignant that I was pushed into something I didn't want to do, and that I was then made to stay there. Even at a young age, I knew that *that* big part of my life was something someone else wanted me to live, and I was not okay with that.

Putting my foot down senior year was one of the most gratifying moments of my youth. I learned that sometimes, when we know what is best for us and our happiness, we *have* to stand up to authority and insist that it will be done our way, come what may.

My senior year was a phenomenal year for me. I joined the choir, began doing what *I* wanted to do, and finally felt that at least some of my life was actually my own.

The Fish Tank

With the exception of a few failed attempts to separate here and there, Eric and I shared a room from the day after he was born until the day I left for college in Hawaii.

Eric has always *loved* fish. As a kid, he would become engrossed in Dad's own hobby for them, and as soon as he was old enough to handle the responsibility of an aquarium, Mom and Dad set him up with a tiny tank in our room. Over the years, he upgraded to bigger and then even bigger aquariums, until we were older teenagers and an entire wall was taken up with this huge 100-gallon beast which held all sorts of cichlids and other large scary looking fresh water fish that he'd been raising for years.

Me, I was a lover of space and design. I have always enjoyed taking whatever space I am living in and making the most of it. This meant *constantly* rearranging our bedroom to try and make things fit better. My hairdresser would tell you that it's because I'm a Gemini. I know better. It's because anything sitting in the same place for very long at all is… boring. How does *everyone* not see that?

Eric always was a good sport when it came to helping me rearrange the room. I think he knew he owed it to me for keeping such a massive *thing* in there that couldn't be moved whenever I had the tinkering to move crap around. Or he could have known that no matter how often he cleaned that *thing*, it always stank at least a little. Or it could be that he knew he owed me for the time he sat on my bed naked, unknowingly farted a Hershey squirt *onto* my sheets, and then blamed his pet iguana when I inadvertently stuck my hand firmly into it. I nearly murdered him that day.

But he lived. And he knew that I never cared all that much for his fish aquariums, or his iguanas, or his chameleons, or the annoyingly loud crickets he kept to feed them. But when you share a room, you learn to give and take.

One day I asked him to help me move the beds around. I had this amazing idea of how we could free up a little extra space for our collection of Sobe bottles. It was an amazing collection. We spent two years buying, emptying, and refilling Sobe bottles with water, and finding awesome places in our room to display them. Mom never did appreciate the art that those bottles were, but we knew that someday they'd be worth a *lot* of money. Today they line the crown molding in her home gym. She loves them now just as much as she did then, and yes, we're still planning to make our fortune off of them.

Anyway, that day we took one of the beds apart since simply scooting them wasn't possible in the space we had. As soon as we lifted the box spring, we realized we had a problem. We had been shoving all sorts of crap under that bed for months. There were dirty clothes, shoes, hangers, garbage, eaten-on dishes, crusty socks (only once-teenage boys will understand that), and I'm pretty sure the skeletal remains of a parakeet or something. Shoving stuff under the beds was an old habit from childhood that really didn't want to die. Any time Mom asked us to clean our room, we'd just bulldoze everything out of sight.

I leaned the mattress and box spring against one wall and Eric leaned the end-boards and side-rails against another, then we got to work cleaning up the mess from underneath both beds.

In the middle of it, Eric had to leave. I don't know where he was headed. Probably to some karate thing. Or breakdancing thing. Or cheerleading thing. Or some other awful thing where he actually found a way to sweat. I don't know why he did that crap. Getting fatter and doing nothing was so much more fun. That was my story, and I was sticking to it.

I told him I'd wait to finish until he got back. I didn't know if he had crusty socks under *his* bed, but I sure wasn't going to clean them up if he did.

And I tried to wait. But… the apparent Gemini in me wasn't having it. Eventually doing nothing in a room that was on the verge of being gloriously *different* became even more boring than furniture that just sat there, so I finished the cleanup myself. Several garbage bags, trips to the kitchen sink, and full laundry hampers later, I emerged barely scathed, only slightly diseased, and ready to move some things around.

I'll be honest. My heart started racing with excitement just writing that last paragraph, that's how much I love rearranged living spaces.

I started by tugging and pushing the one bed that was still assembled to its new location. My parents had bought us all solid oak bed sets with unbelievably thick mattresses, so it was no easy task. Especially on plush carpet. The bed was budging only an inch or two at a time, and I kept getting in front of it and behind it, inching it closer to its next resting place.

Then, it happened.

The incident.

My heel kicked back and bumped one of the side rails that was leaning against the wall. I heard a slow scratching sound and turned around just in time to see the top end of the rail arch directly towards Eric's fish aquarium.

You know how there are those moments in your life where half a second seems more like a minute, and you have no choice but to watch whatever it is happen that you *really* don't want to happen?

The rail smashed through the glass of the aquarium and 100 gallons of dirty water, several large fish, rocks, gravel, plants, and God knows what else, came flooding onto the floor. I can only imagine that the Israelites saw a very similar sight when Moses did his thing after they had crossed the Red Sea, only what I went through was much more terrifying. The Israelites were watching all their problems go away when Moses did that. I was watching a world of hurt land at my feet.

Just as it was sinking in that there were live fish gasping for air and flopping around on all sides of me, I heard Eric say something to Mom upstairs. He was *home*.

And I booked it the hell out of there.

At the other end of the hall was my sisters' bathroom. I bolted inside and quietly shut the door just as I heard him bounding down the stairs.

Then I heard a scream. "What the? Dan! Dan! Dan!" The panic in his voice still rattles me. I didn't know what to do (I mean, you heard me mention that this guy was a master of karate, right?), so from behind the closed bathroom door I yelled back.

"What?!"

He didn't accuse me of anything. He didn't get angry at me. He just called for help. "My fish tank broke! Hurry! Help me! Please!"

I sprang from the bathroom and fastened on the most surprised face I could muster as I rounded the entryway of our now flooded bedroom. "What the hell happened?" I demanded.

He had grabbed a bucket from the closet and was scooping up fish and putting them into it as quickly as he could.

"Help me get the fish!" he screamed. In that moment, the aquarium didn't matter. Only his prized fish did. He had raised those things from tiny little pet store guppies, and I knew very well that he had put a lot of work and money into them.

Once he had collected the fish and run water into the bucket, he came back to survey the rest of the damage. "Do you know what happened?" he asked.

"Dude, I don't know. I was taking a dump and next thing I knew I heard you screaming." There was no way I could man up to the pain that I saw in his eyes. It was brutal. I doubt he'd have eyes like that even at my funeral, that's how much he loved that aquarium and his swimming critters inside.

Then he asked a question that presented me the opportunity to be the biggest schmuck a big brother could be. "One of the side rails fell into it. How would it just fall over?" he quietly said.

I shook my head. "You're the one who leaned them up there. I don't know."

He was too busy solving his problem to see me hang my head in shame.

I learned two things from that experience.

First, I learned that fish are resilient little suckers. Every single fish that spilled out of that aquarium, survived.

Second, I learned that dirty secrets never go away.

Over the years, Eric more or less forgot about it. He'd tell the story from time to time, sure. But he rarely thought about it, and he never dwelled on it.

Me, on the other hand, I thought about it for eleven years. I dwelled on it for eleven years. The guilt of it never left me. For eleven *freaking* years. I had betrayed my brother. I had lied to my best friend. I had failed to own up to something I did to hurt a person that I *really* loved.

He and I didn't have a relationship of dishonesty or mistrust. We told each other everything. We hid nothing from each other.

Well, except this.

And eleven years after the incident, I finally couldn't stomach it any longer. I pulled him aside, and I told him that I needed to confess something to him.

After I revealed to him just who was responsible for the broken tank, he looked at me and forced a weird laugh. He had to, right? It had been eleven years. He told me it was okay. I mean, he had to, right? It had been *eleven* years.

What he couldn't hide was the betrayal that he felt. It poured through his eyes as he processed it the way the fish water had poured through that broken glass.

He didn't care that I had broken his aquarium. He had long ago stopped caring about that.

He cared that I had lied to him. Even though it had been so long that it almost shouldn't have mattered at all.

Rejected

By the end of high school, I had kissed all sorts of girls.

Heather. A spicy little red-head who worked with me at Wendy's took me once after closing to the volcano, a wooden teepee shaped hut at the local playground where all the cool kids went to get their mack on. Heather was both crazy and overly sexual. She would demand what she wanted and then take it whether the other person was comfortable with it or not. I gave my virginity to Heather.

Stacey. A cute little country girl two years younger than I was. We used to sneak out to the playhouse in the backyard at night, strip down to our undies, and roll around on the redwood flooring as we kissed passionately. I never got too crazy with her because she was too much a sweetheart to defile. We kept it to undies and smooching.

Vanessa. A *really* hot Brazilian foreign exchange student who was attending a high school two towns over. We met at a football game and she used to meet me after I got off work for some proper snogging. You know, on the nights when Heather and I weren't off fooling around in the volcano.

Amber was the girl I'd sneak out of class with at school sometimes. Tamara was the girl I'd hook up with after our weekly church youth nights. Amanda was the girl who gave me my first blow job.

At least... these were the stories I told Eric. And my best friends. And my regular friends. And my kind of friends. And my acquaintances. And random horny men pretending to be women in AOL chat rooms.

And they were all completely true. Except that they weren't actually true at all. None of them. Ever.

If Steve Urkel, Lisa Simpson, Chunk from the Goonies, and Steve Buscemi, all got together to have the most awkward, weird, socially deficient kid imaginable, I probably would have been the aftermath of that experiment gone wrong. There was no way any girl anywhere was ever going to kiss me. At least not one that I could brag to my buddies about.

And so I did the next best thing to getting real action. I made up stories about getting real action and I got the kudos for it as if it actually happened. I was such a gifted story teller that I don't think anyone ever doubted me. I learned quickly that I could make up a life that wasn't mine and *instantly* not be thought the loser anymore. After all, only the guys who aren't ugly, and aren't awkward, and aren't shy, and aren't *me* get pretty little wild things competing for their time, attention, and sexual advances.

Looking back, I can honestly say that I don't regret telling those lies.

I was a *really* broken person by the time my last two years of high school rolled around. I didn't believe I was worth anything at all to anyone. I didn't believe I had value. I had no self-esteem. I was angry and bitter toward so many people. And, I hated myself.

I *needed* those lies. And I needed lots of them.

Because I told so many lies, and I told them for so long, and I began receiving the recognition and respect that went along with living such a life at that age, I actually started to *believe* that I was everything I presented myself to be. I started to believe that I had value. And that I was good enough to get pretty girls. And that someone out there would actually want me.

And with that new seed of belief planted, I left home, flew halfway across the Pacific Ocean, and began the next phase of my life: idiot college student.

I stepped off the plane in Hawaii and breathed in a deep lungful of air. It was a new start. *Nobody* here knew who I was before I came to this place. *Nobody* knew that I was shy. Or that I was scared of anything with a vagina. Or that I had never been asked to a girl's choice dance. Or that I thought it was cool to suck air into my butt and blow it back out again. Or that I had conquered the third *Mario Bros.* more than 100 times while pounding pastries and chocolate milk late into the night with my best friend every weekend.

After inhaling my first breath of Hawaiian goodness, I let the island air sit in my lungs for the longest time before I breathed it back out again. Starting right then, I would be the person I had always been in my stories. I would be brave. And bold. And confident. I would find both friends and love the *real* way this time.

I wanted to kiss a girl. I wanted to actually meet a girl, let her be the first person to actually *see* how amazing I was, and press my lips against hers. I wanted to make an honest man of my high school lying self.

And then I met Rachel.

She was a fairly cute, slender and freckled brunette in my English 1010 class. We sat by each other on the first day of school. I spent the entire hour ignoring the instructor while summoning the courage to *say* something to her before the hour was up. Class ended and I didn't say a damned thing. And then I didn't say anything the day after that, either. But on the third day, I finally summoned the courage as she was stuffing her textbooks into her backpack and just before she left I blurted out, "so do you know what you're going to write your essay on?" She laughed and told me she hadn't decided yet, then she walked out of the room. I stood up, puffed my chest out, and acknowledged to the world and to myself (silently, of course) that I was now a champion.

Things actually began going very well with Rachel after that. We started chatting before and after classes. We started walking from classes together. We started sitting together in the cafeteria. We started studying together. We started going to visit and see things on the island together. We eventually even started holding hands, and hugging, and snuggling up against each other.

One afternoon, after weeks of ever-growing intimacy, we stood on the sidewalk outside her dorms. She had both of her hands in mine and was swaying back and forth as we talked. Toward me. And away from me. Toward me. And away from me.

Every time she swayed forward she brought her face a little closer toward mine.

She wanted to be kissed.

And she didn't just want to be kissed. She wanted *me* to kiss her.

Toward me. And away from me. Forward. Back. Closer. And closer. And closer.

I could have gone for it.

I could have laid a big, wet, sloppy first kiss on her and she would have kissed me back. I've had first kisses with enough women now to know that with certainty.

Every part of me longed to just go for it. I didn't move even though every nerve in every muscle of my body was firing in an attempt to both push me toward her and pull myself away.

My mind raced in a thousand different directions. Every time she came closer to me, I played out a new scenario of what would happen if I went for it and she pulled away. Or what would happen if I went for it, and she slapped me. Or what would happen if I went for it, and I had misread the entire thing. Never once did I think about what would happen if I went for it and she actually kissed me back.

And so, I took the coward's approach and at a mental stand-off I asked her, "is it okay if I kiss you?"

It was safe. She would say yes. And we would kiss. I felt suddenly confident the moment I heard the words unexpectedly escape my lips.

Instead of saying yes, though, she began laughing hysterically and after she stopped laughing, she replied with a simple "no" and began laughing again.

I dropped her hands and I looked at her in a way that said, *you are by far the vilest and meanest woman on this planet.* I fought off tears as my throat began to close off. She saw the look on my face and went silent.

And then she did the worst thing a person can do in such an awkward situation. She tried to explain why she had told me no.

"You don't ever *ask* a girl if you can kiss her," she said. "A real man just goes for it."

I didn't know enough about myself or about women to know that I hadn't lost my chance for a kiss at that point. I hadn't lost her, or her affection for me. I didn't know that I had simply done something that she thought was funny, she had laughed, and she wanted me to be more of a man about it.

And with *really* hurt feelings I told her I needed to go. I'd see her later.

And I walked away.

I *walked away* from a pretty girl that I really liked and who really liked me so that I could... *brood?* So that I could... be *sad?* So that I could... *what* exactly?

As I walked away I did so knowing that it was over. I did so knowing that her rejection was the end of our relationship. It was the ultimate sign that she, just like every other girl I had fallen for since my first childhood love, *couldn't* love me. I was too fat. I was too awkward. I was too *not* the guy every girl obviously wanted.

It took me years before I understood what actually had happened between Rachel and me that day, and the lessons I have carried from that have been profound.

I eventually learned that our relationship with each other didn't end when she rejected me. It also didn't end when I asked her if I could kiss her.

It ended when I walked away and let myself *believe* that I wasn't good enough to be what Rachel desired. The moment I let that thought enter my head, it was over between us. It was the beginning of a rapidly approaching and inevitable demise that I conjured from nowhere.

After that, I began backing up my own self-doubting beliefs with proof that I somehow was able to find everywhere I turned my gaze. Within days I had disproved to myself every good thing Rachel and I ever were together. I had convinced myself that none of it was sincere. And I soon started ignoring her completely.

Deep down, no matter how fresh a start I declared that I deserved, I felt I wasn't worthy of being loved, and so I let the first chance I ever had at real love bounce off of whatever filter it is that makes humans do that.

And, guess what. Humans everywhere play that self-destructing mental game *all the time.* "We accept the love we think we deserve." I love that line from *The Perks of Being a Wallflower.* I would also rephrase it to say "We reject the love we don't think we deserve." The difference is subtle, but it's important, and both statements are annoyingly and disgustingly true.

It would take me years to learn that more often than not, the greatest thing standing between me and life's greatest moments is fear. The only thing standing between me and real love is usually fear. And the only thing standing between me and the happiness I long so deeply for is *fear.*

I will always only be able to be as happy as I believe I should be.

We *all* will always only be able to be as happy as we believe we should be. We will only be as successful as we believe we can be. And we will only be as loved as we believe we deserve to be.

Fear of rejection. Fear of dismissal. Fear of not being wanted or needed. These are the fears that stop us from having all that we want in our lives. These are the fears that stop us from having the love we long for so constantly. It is these fears that take away the chance at almost every good thing that could otherwise be ours.

Yes. The greatest lesson I learned is that when we act out of fear, we will almost always lose that which we fear losing the most. And we will lose it because we will *make* ourselves lose it. This is, very unfortunately, human nature.

Had I found the courage and simply gone in for that kiss, I'd have a very different story to tell today. She would have kissed me back, we would have laughed together about that, and our relationship would have carried on.

Oh, it would have ended sooner than later, I'm sure. Overcoming the voices and the demons from our pasts is never as simple as taking in a giant lungful of island air and declaring that we are leaving the past behind. But I would have had a different story to tell about *that* moment and I would have had that single story of bravery to push me forward along the path to healing instead of yet another story of rejection to pull me back harder along the path of self-doubt.

Rejection is a part of life. Even the best and most confident of us will experience it many times. What will define that rejection is whether we let it define us or not. Will we go in for that kiss or not? When the kiss doesn't happen, will we walk away deflated or will we walk away indifferent? And will we try again the next time, or not?

I can tell you this much. Rarely will anything deservedly great happen when we allow our instinctual fears to dictate what our next moves will be. In fact, one of the only ways to truly guarantee failure is to simply fail to try. Why I have had to relearn this concept so many times, and will most certainly have to be taught it repeatedly through what life I have left, is proof of what a difficult truth it really can be.

Tenniele

In the aftermath of Rachel, the insecurity ghosts of my adolescence began howling really ugly things in my ear. And I'm talking hideous Thanksgiving turtleneck ugly. "Yoooooou are unlovable. Yoooooooou can't get a girlfriend. Noooooooo girl will genuinely like yooooou. Your feet loooooooooook like they have bat wings built onto them." (You've got to read that in your head like a ghost would. Or at least how *my* ghosts would.)

Yes. After Rachel, each day I seemed to talk myself into liking myself even less than the day before. I became consumingly homesick, and my thoughts began spiraling in so many new and dark directions.

While on that island, I wrote weekly letters to my family. The Internet was still fairly new, and while email existed, I still preferred the hand-written stuff most of the time. In my letters, I told them all of my going-ons, my classes, and my friends. I shared some of my honest struggles and triumphs, and sent home photos as often as I could.

But for some reason, I never sent home *anything* about Rachel. No photos. No quick mentions of, "hey, there's this awesome new chick in my life." I think some big part of me never wanted to tell them about this amazing girl because I knew very well that botching it with her was inevitable. A big part of me knew I was too cowardly and insecure to make the relationship last. I suppose it could have been the scared part of me that, oh, I don't know… was continuously obsessed with how I had so quickly bungled it with each and every girl since that first childhood wart-hiding love.

And then, about two weeks after Rachel, I met Tenniele.

Tenniele was gorgeous. 5'10". She was a full-blooded Hawaiian, yet slender-boned and thin like a white movie star. She had ample bosoms. She was big into surfing. She had a laugh and a brightness that could pleasantly melt a tub of gravel. She was kind to *everyone*. She loved to dance. She loved to sing. She volunteered wherever she could. She loved animals. She loved her large family.

And she loved *me*.

She loved everything about me. She wanted me as much as I wanted her. And we had *quickly* fallen in love. We spent our days on the beach doing homework together. She was teaching me how to surf. One time her surfboard got stuck in a cave and I went to rescue it for her. She rewarded me by tackling me, pinning me into the sand, and kissing me passionately. She didn't care about my weight. She didn't care about my awkward looks. She was, in a word, flawless.

And I *did* write to my family about Tenniele. I told them of our great adventures and our moments of wild romance. I sent photos of her. I asserted my love for this girl every chance I had. If Facebook would have been around back then, I would have driven everyone crazy with walls full of the gooey eye-rolling stories behind our whirlwind romance.

In fact, Tenniele was so close to perfect that I can honestly say she had only one teeny tiny flaw.

Okay, it was a huge flaw.

Tenniele wasn't real.

And I'm not saying that in the kumbaya, everyone *be real* sense that people like me love to rant on about. I'm not saying it in the kind of *be real* sense that this book and the stories within are ultimately centered around. I literally mean that she wasn't real. As in, she didn't exist.

Just like that, I was back to my old high school lying-and-making-up-pretty-girl ways.

In the thick of my greatest insecurities, I had *invented* someone else out of thin air to love me. Only this time, I took it much further than I ever had before.

I *created* a fake human so that nobody else in the whole world would see just how big a loser I really was. I designed a fictitious love because I still, even after leaving home and flying across an ocean, could not find a real one.

And I'm telling you, if there was an award for epic lying, I would have won it. I went out of my way to support the illusion. I told story after story, connecting each to the last. I downloaded photos of some aspiring Polynesian model I found on the internet, printed them off, and sent them home, attached to my hand-written letters. And the more I sent, the more attached I got to my fake scenario and my fake girlfriend because... people *liked* Tenniele. People were giving *me* big kudos for finding such an awesome girl. People were telling me that I deserved something so amazing in my life. Mom and Dad would write back about meeting her someday. Eric repeatedly told me how gorgeous she was and how jealous he was. I had pulled the wool over their eyes, and I had no intentions of ever taking it off. Not when I was getting that kind of attention. Not when nobody knew or suspected the truth.

The truth that said, I *thoroughly* believe I'm such a dud that no real girl would ever actually fall for me. The truth that said, I had given up and was laying alone in my dorm room every night watching *Tommy Boy* on repeat. The truth that said, my *only* real friends in Hawaii were my right hand and the dude I bought weekly roach traps from at the convenience store. The truth that said, happiness for me will only ever exist in a fantasy world. The truth that said, smoked gouda is never as good as plain gouda, and hairless dogs are the most awkward breathing things in domestic existence.

I saw no harm in keeping the ruse going. I was out on an island in the middle of an ocean. Nobody was going to fly out there and call me out on it. Nobody had any way of verifying anything. As long as I kept control of every detail I could keep it going, and... *end* the story any way I wanted.

I knew that I would be transferring to Southern Utah University the following semester, so eventually I began planning and plotting the finale of our (so far) faultless love affair.

I could kill Tenniele off perhaps? Say my girlfriend got hit by a stray torpedo from a rogue Mongolian submarine while she was surfing? No, too drastic. They wouldn't believe it. She got hit by a pineapple truck? No, definitely not. Mom and Dad might love me enough to fly out and support me through her funeral services. She cheated on me with a gorgeous blue-eyed Scandinavian underwear model, so I gave her the boot? That wouldn't work, either. Tenniele was too perfect to do something like that. She loved me *too* much to ever betray me. No, I had to find a way to end it in a way that left me looking like a super stud and kept the perfect girlfriend illusion in place.

I thought I had a couple months to work that part of it out. I had every intention of "dating" Tenniele until the end of the semester. But something terrifying started to happen.

People started asking specific questions about it. About her. About me. About us.

Mom started asking me how I felt about leaving Tenniele behind when I transfer back to Utah. Eric began asking me about things like upcoming weekend plans. Dad asked me if I was sure I wanted to leave Hawaii when I had something so good and positive going for me.

It didn't take long to realize that it wasn't a harmless fantasy. It was what it was. A blatant lie.

It was exciting and fun for me when all anyone replied were things like, "go get 'em Mr. Awesome!" and "you're the freaking stud ball of the decade!" That part of it was so rewarding, and lasted for a few emboldening weeks. But when people started pushing for more details something else happened, unexpectedly. To keep the fantasy alive, I would have to start giving everyone else control of it. I would have to answer *their* questions with lies. The story could go in a hundred different directions, none of which would be mine and all of which would begin to conflict with one another. I would not be able to contain it.

As undeniably stupid as I was at 18, I was smart enough to realize that to take it any further would weave such a tangled web that eventually it would blow up in my face. Big time.

In a matter of days, I began hating the original story; the original lie. I hated that I had made it up at all. There was no taking it back. To admit that I lied would do two things. It would push everyone to think the exact thoughts I was trying to avoid by inventing Tenniele in the first place, and it would unveil that I was a dirty, rotten deceiver.

And so, I ended things with Tenniele in the only way I knew everyone would believe and let go of without further questioning.

She lost interest in me.

She couldn't love me.

And she moved on.

That's what I told them. And just like I knew would be the case, nobody doubted it.

Tenniele was *definitely* too good for a guy like me to hold onto.

I've still never admitted the truths behind Tenniele to anyone in my family. The first they will hear about it is when they read this memoir, along with the rest of the world. Over the years, they still ask me about her from time to time. They still mention her. They ask me every now and then if I've ever found her on Facebook. I just dodge the question and find a way to point the subject elsewhere.

There are three major lessons I've carried with me since my glorious days with that perfect Hawaiian girl.

I've learned to preemptively cover up my lies better so that it never gets to the point where I can't keep them going.

That was a joke. Chill out.

But seriously, three life truths.

I learned that significant lies will always beget more lies. What starts as something simple to cover up an insecurity will snowball until containing it becomes impossible. This snowball is inexorable and certain.

I also learned that the need to be loved is so real that inherently good people will do things they never otherwise would to try and make it somehow exist. I didn't fabricate the story of that girl to have fun at the expense of others. I lied because I needed to believe that I was lovable. I lied because I needed to know that other people *believed* I was lovable. I lied because being loved in my imagination was somehow as powerful as being loved by a real person.

And perhaps more than anything, I learned that in the long run I will never *actually* believe any of the respect, love, and admiration others given me in the wake of my lies if it isn't real, coming from real people. I certainly will never trust it long term, so long as it is founded on something without integrity. All accolades will be more hollow than a gutted fish and they'll stink twice as bad. They will drain my self-esteem bucket faster than they will ever be able to fill it because in the end I now have two ugly truths to sit on. The original truth that I was trying to obscure, and the new truth. The truth that I am a liar and a coward, afraid of his own reality.

And who wants to be *that?*

Missing Shoes

And now, a short and pointless little story from a different time in my life, with an even more pointless moral attached to it. The year: 2015.

"Oh my God. My shoes. I think I left my shoes at the hotel!"

I was suddenly panicked, where moments before I was content as a stinkbug on an overcooked hamburger patty to be headed back to the airport and back to real life. It had been a long, much-needed escape full of booze, best friends, cruise ship shenanigans, and over-eager Mexican street hustlers. We had done the trip right, from beginning to end, and now we were headed to LAX, sharing a common desire to get back to our kids, routines, healthy living, and at *least* six booze-free hangover-free years to follow.

Usually a pair of shoes wouldn't be enough to make me, and an entire car full of burnt-out people, drive an hour out of our way to retrieve them. But these weren't just any shoes. They had been given to me as a gift, and were nicer than just about anything in my wardrobe by a couple hundred bucks at least.

"Can you pull over really quick?" I wasn't really asking. "I need to check my suitcase. I don't think they're in there, but they could be," I said, praying with all my agnostic little heart that I was simply forgetting altogether having packed them. I *knew* I hadn't grabbed them, though. I had just barely packed my luggage in the final moments before we left, and I recalled very specifically putting each and every item inside because it took more concentration than a high-speed game of Tetris to make it all fit, and quickly.

My friend pulled the car over onto a side street lined with hoary, yet pleasant little bungalows. *Maybe my shoes somehow got kicked under the bed...* I didn't know. My mind was a blur with thought of where I might have left them. *Maybe they were shoved behind the curtains.* But I had done a careful sweep of the hotel room for anything left behind. I would have seen them, surely.

I could sense the tension and apprehension in the faces of my travel companions. Losing an hour when they had to get me to the airport, and when they wanted to get started on their own road trip home, was less than an ideal thought. Yet, they were good friends and neither griped nor protested.

"Pop the trunk!" I yelled, as I exited. The rear of the car soon gaped open, allowing me to dig in and explore my way to the bad news I knew was certain.

Come on, come on, just be in there.

I yanked my oversized suitcase from the car, and set it on the pavement.

I unzipped it.

And with far less care than I should have given for how meticulously it was originally packed, I opened it up and began rummaging.

Nothing.

I searched it again, leaving no further order to what was left inside.

The shoes weren't there.

I sat back on the strength of my own burning quadriceps, trying to decide if I should wave the white flag and just leave them behind, or if I should inconvenience everyone, and possibly even miss my flight home to go back for them. *No shoes left behind,* and all that jazz.

It really was a question of time.

I looked down at my watch, ready to do some heavy calculation and quick decision-making.

And right then, I saw them.

My shoes.

My *missing* shoes.

The shoes over which my heart had nearly just exploded.

Both there.

On my... *feet.*

I was wearing the damn things the entire time.

Well, this is a little embarrassing.

I crammed my suitcase shut, threw it in the trunk, hopped in the car again, and slammed the door behind me.

"Did you find them?" my friends both said in unison.

"Yep."

Relief flooded both their faces.

"Oh, good!" came the reply. "Where were they?!"

I dramatically looked down at my shoes. I looked up at my friends again and smirked. "Just drive," I said. "Just drive."

Pointless moral of the story: Sometimes the first place you should go looking for something is the last and most obvious place it probably is.

And with that, we'll get back to it...

The Spot

I shed a great deal of the fat by the time I transferred to SUU the semester following Hawaii. And by a great deal, I mean 79 lbs. How that happened in two and a half months could make a great science fiction book all by itself, and there was absolutely nothing healthy in the way I pulled it off. Just know that after the Tenniele façade came to a close, I was determined, at any cost, to transfer over to my next school a transfigured person. I would have gnawed my own ass cheeks off if it would have made that happen. There was no way I was going to be that same guy who Rachel obviously never wanted, and who Tenniele clearly was too good for, when I stepped off that plane again.

It was going to be a new start of a new life for me. This was more or less the exact same thought I had when stepping off the plane in Hawaii, I know. And, yes. It was just as positively cliché as the first time I thought it. I also meant it both times.

The driving forces behind the extremeness which led to the unhealthy weight-loss were a cocktail of desperation and hopefulness, splashed with a sense of inordinate urgency to *get on already* with the fucking awesome life I just knew I was designed to live.

My same-age cousin was already going to school there, and had committed me to join him by promising that the hard work was already done when it came to the most important thing in all of life.

Girls.

He had exciting and substantial friendships already established with a harem of young, hot, horny female freshman. He wasn't full of hot air, either. He would send (real) photographs and tell me (real) stories of his (real) adventures with them. I'd get online from 2,878 miles away and chat late into the night with many of the gals in his dormitories, and for only fifteen cents an hour! Over the course of two months, and hundreds of screeching modems later, I became good friends with many of them. I was – quite assuredly this time – making the move straight from loser past and into the glorious future. So long as I wasn't some huge fat ass when I did, I just might have a shot at love sticking around the next time I happened to wallow into it.

I moved into B-Hall of the school dormitories. It was filled with the most fascinating group of teenage boys with whom I had ever been in constant and close proximity. There was Green, who I quickly learned to latch onto because he always was somehow surrounded by all the ladies. There was Indian Jimmy who sat in his dorm room eating corn chips, playing video games all day most days. He wasn't to be confused with Big Jimmy, the guy who lived in the dorm across the hall who had the notoriously biggest penis any of us had ever laid eyes on. And believe me, he had no trouble whipping that thing out and showing it off every chance he got. Then there was Fat Curtis. He introduced me to my first alcoholic beverage ever: peach schnapps. I took one sip of it and felt like the biggest badass of all time. There were a couple real jerks who lived down the hall. They were far too cool to let themselves be associated with the rest of us.

And then there was me and my cousin Glen, sharing a room which we turned into party central. We built our own giant wooden contraption that held one bed inside the other so that we could fit a couch against the opposite wall where the other bed used to be. We had the biggest TV of anyone there, the DVD player (hey, they were new and impressive back then), *and* we had the best video game system. Over in one corner was a lava lamp. In the other, party lights. Hanging on the interior side of the door was a necktie which, when hung on the outside of a shut door, meant "don't come in. I'm getting it on in here."

Our room was strategic and perfect, so long as you don't count the ever-emanating stench of flatulence, sweat, and semen that hit you when you neared the threshold.

Still, we had nonstop girls over. I never made out with any of them at first. I still had no idea how to go about it. But we played lots of kissing games, watched lots of movies, and began our journey toward flunking out of school (which we both did with gusto that semester). Judging by how often the necktie was never tied on the outside of the door, I don't think my cousin ever got lucky with anyone either. But the system was there, *just in case.*

Most of the girls came from A-Hall. The girls in those dorms were my first taste of female crazy. They were exciting. They were just as life-stupid and reckless as we were. And we all loved having absurd fun together. There was Shandy. She became the best friend who never mixed pleasure and business. She took her make-outs outside of B Hall. There was Katrina #1 who my cousin supposedly made out with all the time. I just never saw it. Pink and Clara lived down the hall and they used to hang with us and have a blast with us, but they were *very* good Mormon girls who never got into any real trouble. There was Janice, my cousin's ex-girlfriend who seemed to have a thing for me from day one, but with whom I could never hook up because I was too faithful to my cuz (yeah, we'll go with that story). And then there was Katrina #2.

Katrina #2 was a good looking girl. She was one of the girls I had chatted with while I was in Hawaii. And something just clicked between us when I got there. We started hanging out in each other's dorm rooms regularly, and one day while we lay on her bed laughing, I just went for it without thinking. The kiss.

I'd never done it before and as I zeroed in, I had a panic attack and hesitated. *What if she didn't want to kiss me back? What if this move would blow everything with her?* She sensed my awkward vacillation and asked what the matter was. I just looked back at her with giant frightened eyes. I still remember my eyebrow twitching in that moment. *Shit. This is Rachel all over again. It's happening again. It's happening again. What do I do now? Abort? Abort!*

Lucky for me, Katrina was much more experienced in such matters than I was, and she finished the job before I could retreat.

Cowardice 1. Dan 0.

She lunged at me and suddenly we were full-fledge making out.

I had never even kissed a girl outside of spin the bottle and other such games for college youngsters. But I knew exactly what to do. After all, I had fantasized about it more times than I could count.

We just kissed forever, laying on the bed with each other, hardly touching at all. And then, I learned something. When a tongue comes out, and you're in college, and you're on a dorm room bed, things can progress very quickly.

French kissing was not what I thought it would be. Katrina had a barbell through her tongue, which was both awe-inspiring and terrifying. She was a fabulous kisser. I *think*. I honestly had absolutely nothing to compare it to. But I went with it. And when she stuck her tongue in my mouth, I stuck my tongue in hers.

That part was *weird*. I'm not prideful enough to say otherwise. Our tongues were both slimy and slippery and slobbery. I could very potently taste the Tootsie Roll she had just eaten. As it turns out, leftover Tootsie Roll slime coming from someone else's mouth is gross. No need to try it. Just take my word for it.

But, hey. I was *French kissing* a girl. So who the hell cared? We began pulling each other closer and tighter, and we began rolling around together, suddenly our crotches were pressing into each other, and then...

She sat up on the bed, pulled her shirt off faster than I could think an impure thought about it, and began reaching for her bra.

Holy shit. I'd dreamed of this moment so many times before, but now that it was here I was scared as hell about what was coming. Was this something I really wanted? Was it something I was ready for?

At this point, the thought of actual sex was not anywhere on my mind. I had no idea that college girls even had sex. Not in Utah. We were all Mormons, just having fun doing things that were bad, but not *bound for hell* bad. And sex wasn't on her mind either. She just wanted me to play with her breasts, and as she reached for her bra, I realized, *I'm scared, but yeah, I really do want this.*

"Have you ever felt a pair of Double D's?" she said as she pushed the button on the front of her bra and it burst open, exposing two fantastic and beautiful God-made boobs. Her nipples were hard and tightened by the coolness of her room. They seemed to point straight at me, commanding me in all things I should do next.

"Nope," was all I could squeak out, and I reached up and took her breasts in my hands.

No sooner did I make contact with them than I ejaculated in my pants.

I didn't feel it coming, and I certainly wasn't expecting it. I held perfectly still, acted like I was just pausing to savor the moment, and when the orgasm was over, we continued making out as if nothing had happened.

To this day, I don't know if she knew that I creamed my drawers.

What I *do* know is that I never felt so manly as when I went back to my room that night, violently swung open the door, and *so* proudly showed my cousin the wet spot on my jeans.

I was too naïve to know that men all over the world felt insecure and vulnerable about their premature ejaculation struggles. I had no idea that it was something guys and girls alike poke fun at. I had no clue that it was considered a weakness at all, and by the vast majority of others, at that.

All I knew was that I had finally done something I had always been too scared to do, and it had led to the most glorious fifteen minutes of my life. I had *kissed* a girl. Like, *really* kissed her. I had *French* kissed that girl. I had tasted that chocolatey slime. I had played with the piercing in her tongue. I had *touched* her breasts. I had fondled them, and had had them in my mouth! In that moment, I did not care at all that I had just done something considered heinous within the religion I was raised. I did not care at all that I had ended things early with my little how-do-you-do surprise. I was *not* that fat loser who couldn't get a girl. Not anymore. And the proof was right there in my pants. Dark, and wet, and gooey, and exultantly gross.

That day I learned a really valuable truth in such an unexpected way. I learned that what to one man is weakness, to another man just might be glorious.

I learned that as people, we really can't compare our triumphs to those of another because we don't know what kind of battles they may have fought to get as far as they have.

We also can't compare our failures to those of another, because we don't ever actually know if their failures are actually failures for them at all.

I also learned that we can't ever compare our triumphs and failures of today to those of our past. What right now for me would most certainly be a failure, might long ago have been a great victory or triumph. Life is one giant progression for every person. It is the very personal evolution of both learning and experience, and I assure you, it's all relative. Always.

Believe me. I would have *preferred* to have a different story to tell you all *how* I learned this life lesson, but life comes at you how it will. If we listen to what's being taught, we'll often learn in the strangest moments of all. Such was the case with me, and the glorious spot in my pants.

Breaking Windows

I always considered myself to be an overly rebellious kid. But a single event during that same semester of college made me realize that I actually wasn't that rebellious at all.

I believe I was actually a defiant kid. I learned this when I found myself stuck in the back seat of a pickup truck, with a group of friends who decided we were going to spend our evening driving around town, vandalizing other people's property.

Defiant kids just don't like authority, and they don't like being told things have to be a certain way. They argue. They go do the things that authority figures tell them they shouldn't be doing because *they* know when the authority figures have it wrong.

A defiant kid disagrees with many things, but he also agrees with other things. He uses logic and reasoning to decide what he is going to do or not do.

An example of a defiant kid is one whose parents tell him he can't stay out past curfew, but he does anyway because it's prom, dammit, and every kid should be able to stay out later on prom night.

Rebellious kids, they just like to go against anything and everything that anyone tells them to do. They like to push their limits with social norms, drugs and alcohol, and even more weighty things like the law.

A rebellious kid disagrees with pretty much everything that *anyone* in an authority position tells him is right or that he must do or not do. He doesn't use a whole lot of logic or reasoning to decide what his next actions are once authority has dictated. He just does the opposite, and often thrives on the attention that derives from it.

An example of a rebellious kid is one whose parents tell him he can't stay out past curfew on prom night, but he does anyway, and he gets shit-faced drunk, has crazy sex, and tells his parents the next day that he doesn't have to listen to such crazy prudes who are stuck in the mindset of previous generations. Then he posts pictures online of his debaucheries, just to get under his parents' skin all the more.

I was definitely defiant. Not rebellious.

On *my* prom night, I sat in the car talking to my prom date, pressed against the opposite door, overly careful not to let anything happen that would make my parents right. I kept looking at the clock just to make sure I was staying out later than I was supposed to. I had a point to prove. Mom and Dad were insistent that staying out past curfew led to problems and sin. Drinking. Sex. Drugs. Those were the big ones. My defiant nature pushed me to prove that I *could* stay out late, and it certainly wouldn't lead to *anything* like that. I know, I was a badass.

It also helped immensely that I was still scared to death of girls in high school.

And the night I learned the difference between rebellion and defiance was one of the scariest of my life.

Not too long after my glorious shortcoming (pun definitely intended), a few guys from B Hall invited me to go on a midnight run to McDonald's.

The driver of the pickup truck was Justin. He was a big ass beefcake of a man, even compared to me. He came from some small town outside of Cedar City where the vast majority of every man's vocabulary was made up of short one-word phrases such as "sunuvabitch," "mutherfucker," or "mmmmhmm." He wore cowboy hats, and even at 18 he chewed tobacco. Justin's very existence always made me uneasy but over the short time I was a student there we had struck up the starts of a potential friendship.

Riding shotgun that night was Indian Jimmy. He was in the same boat I was. A little shy. New to the dorms. Fibbed to everyone about his sexual exploits. And happy to be invited anywhere.

I volunteered to be in the back of the extended cab alongside Big Jimmy, who was well known for his DVD mail fraud scams, pimpled face, and as you may remember, his larger than life manhood.

We went through the McDonald's drive-through and ordered our grease-filled bags of college-appropriate food, and we all dug in as Justin started back toward the dorms.

Suddenly, just as I stuffed a handful of over-salted fries into my mouth, he pulled the truck over. "Should we do one?" he said to Big Jimmy who was in the back seat cramming a Big Mac into the hole above his scrawny long neck.

Big Jimmy shoved his burger back into the bag and grinned. "Hell yes," he said and he immediately reached deep into his front jeans pocket.

He pulled out a prescription bottle and started shaking it up and down, listening to the contents rattle.

"What the hell is that?" I demanded in a passively aggressive jovial tone. I'd never done drugs or popped pills before, and I wasn't about to start. Even at a young age I overly valued my brain cells.

Big Jimmy laughed. "It's porcelain."

Justin grunted. "*Mmmmhmmm.*"

Indian Jimmy didn't say anything.

"Porcelain?" I said. "What do you mean?"

Big Jimmy went on to explain that they had gone to some field outside of town where people like to dump their junk. They found an old abandoned toilet, and had smashed that sucker to bits with a sledgehammer. I just shook my head. I had no idea what he was getting at.

He popped the lid off the orange bottle and shook a few small jagged white pieces of toilet into his hand, then held one out to me.

I took it from him, becoming more confused by the moment. "Why do you want porcelain?" I asked as I studied it. It weighed almost nothing, and seemed rather lacking in any purpose I could think of.

"Because," he continued as he suddenly whipped out a wrist rocket slingshot from seemingly nowhere. "When you shoot one at a car window, it shatters into a million pieces instantly."

That was when I got scared. Shit like that surely got you thrown in jail. I didn't say anything. I just swallowed and continued rolling the piece of porcelain back and forth between my thumb and index finger. I didn't see how something so tiny and almost weightless could shatter a window, but I had learned long before not to doubt the foolish antics other teenagers discover and promulgate.

"Watch this," he said. I shook my head again with a scowl growing on my face. Justin grunted something in the front seat and placed his hands on the steering wheel.

Big Jimmy rolled his window down, loaded his wrist rocket with a single tiny piece of porcelain, and pulled it back. "This is the coolest fucking thing you'll ever see."

The only words I really got out were mumbled and squeaky. "Guy's, I think I want to get out." Nobody heard me. If they did, they pretended they didn't.

Before I even finished saying the words, Big Jimmy released the stretched surgical tubing that was holding his little porcelain projectile, and as quickly as it snapped forward, the back window of a parked silver Honda Civic shattered into smithereens and vanished before our very eyes. I had never seen anything like it. And I don't think Indian Jimmy had, either. We both looked at each other worriedly. Justin punched the gas, and we fled the scene of our crime.

Big Jimmy started whoopin' and hollerin' like he had just spun exactly a dollar on *The Price is Right* wheel. Justin joined in, snorting and laughing and saying things like "you ballsy mutherfucker" and "shit on my balls, that was good." He liked to add the word "balls" into most everything he said.

I thought we were done. I hoped we were done. We weren't.

Justin pulled up to another car a couple miles over, and Big Jimmy destroyed another rear window. Again we roared off into the night. I slid down deep in my seat and prayed to find the words that would help get me out of it. By the looks of it, Indian Jimmy was doing the same. We were seconds from being slammed onto the ground in handcuffs. I just knew it.

"You guys try one!"

Justin shouted it as a command more than an offer.

I just looked at him. "I'm good man. I don't wanna do that crap."

"Suit yerself," he said and held his open hand out toward his more criminal friend. Big Jimmy placed the wrist rocket and a piece of porcelain into it. Justin set the weapon in his lap and kept driving.

He didn't ever stop, and eventually headed back toward our dorms.

Thank God, I thought as he parked his truck, and our night of crime came to an end.

We all grabbed our half eaten McDonald's and started our trek inside. My fries were cold, but I had lost my appetite so I didn't really care.

Suddenly Justin stopped walking. He set his food on the ground, loaded the wrist rocket with his piece of porcelain, and he launched it straight at the back window of a red sedan parked outside our dormitories.

As the glass shattered and disappeared, he and Big Jimmy began laughing hysterically, and they both immediately sprinted toward the entrance of the building. Indian Jimmy and I followed their lead and we all ducked inside, undetected.

I was done. "Later," I said as Justin and Big Jimmy hooted and high-fived. Indian Jimmy was already disappearing into his own room.

Without another word, I slipped quietly into mine, closed the door behind me, and sat on the edge of my bed in silence for at least the next half hour.

No part of that had been fun for me. Those were people's cars they were messing with. It was people's paychecks. It was people's safety.

The longer I sat, the angrier I got. They had put me in a bad situation. They had put Indian Jimmy in a bad situation. They had brought their vandalistic tomfoolery onto our home turf.

And they were *laughing* about it. I think that's what bugged me the most. They had no remorse for it. They didn't care who it affected and how. They didn't care about anything, really. They were rebels without a cause, and I finally understood that term.

Before college, my brother and I would join in with our other friends and hit unsuspecting vehicles with water balloons. We'd doorbell ditch our neighbors. We'd toilet paper other people's houses. Hell, once we stole and stockpiled toilet paper for six months and then toilet papered the entire street.

This, though... This was different. This wasn't fun. At all. This really *affected* people.

The next morning, I woke up feeling slightly better about life. We hadn't gotten caught. Cops hadn't come pounding on my door during the night as I had feared they might. I had learned my lesson, and simply wouldn't go anywhere with Justin or Big Jimmy again. It was a Saturday. It was a good day to go have fun with different friends and shake it all off.

I pulled on a pair of board shorts (hey, it was cool back then, and yes, so was free-balling it) and a t-shirt, donned some flip-flops, and stepped out into the hallway. Tall Curtis was standing in the corridor looking perplexed. He spun around and immediately blurted out, "do you know anything about people breaking car windows last night?" My heart tried to retreat into itself, and I forced myself to keep my cool.

Tall Curtis lived three doors to the east of me. We had hung out several times. We talked and laughed and joked every time we saw each other. He played for the school basketball team, was perhaps a little introverted, and in general he was a really nice guy.

"No, why?" I said as innocently as I could.

He groaned. "My girlfriend was hanging out last night, and when she went back out her car window was smashed in. The cops said it happened to other cars around town, too. I know you guys went out. You didn't see anything? You don't know anything?" He was angry. And somehow I sensed that he knew we had something to do with it.

"Sorry man, I have no idea. We went out, but I didn't see anything." I swallowed hard. "That really sucks, dude. I'm sorry."

I didn't know why I was lying. I hadn't done anything wrong. I didn't break the windows. I didn't plot it, or go smash the toilet, or drive around recklessly wreaking havoc. And still, I felt responsible. And I worried about what Big Jimmy or Justin would do if they found out I squealed. So I lied.

And Tall Curtis knew I was lying. I don't know if he saw it in my face, or if he knew something before he asked me, but he knew.

And he wouldn't talk to me the rest of the semester.

I lost a real friend that day, and I learned something.

Losing *real* friends hurts.

As the semester went on, I resented Justin and Big Jimmy more every single day. Nothing else ever happened with them. I never saw them vandalize anything else or cause any more problems. They never tried to make me feel small for not enjoying their illegal fun. I just resented them because they put me in a place where I lied, and my decision to lie made another friend not trust me or like me anymore.

Justin and Big Jimmy were not my real friends. They were fleeting friends. They were friends that could have disappeared, and I honestly probably wouldn't have noticed.

My silence on their behalf did nothing to help our fleeting friendship, and it did everything to destroy what I had and could have had with Tall Curtis and his girlfriend.

At some point, as Tall Curtis passed me for the twentieth time without saying a word or even acknowledging my existence, I made a vow that I would never put my fleeting friends over my real ones. I would never again lie to a real friend to cover up for a reckless one. And I would never again keep my mouth shut to protect the guilty.

Because, you see, real friends are not easy to come by. Fleeting friends are a dime a dozen. And it's never worth sacrificing our real friends for the fleeting ones. When we do that, we tend to end up with no friends at all.

Ratted Out

And just that quickly, another short and pointless little story from a different time in my life, with an even more pointless moral attached to it. The year: 2012.

One of the big three networks (who shall not be named so that I don't get the skivvies sued off of me) was putting me through a rigorous screening process as they sized me up for a role on a reality television show which would compete with that TV show *The Bachelor*.

Yes, I know, I'm not *Bachelor* material. I don't have chiseled abs, 7% body fat, or the ability to make 2 dozen women trip over their four-inch heels in an attempt to catch my overly eager eye. But this wasn't *The Bachelor*. It was a show to *compete* with The Bachelor. Their angle was that they wanted to have real, every day people on it that were "somewhat good looking but not impossibly good looking." They had recruited me to audition, but they didn't choose me.

I *know* that means I wasn't even good looking enough to be considered somewhat good looking. I *choose* to believe that it means I was too good looking for their show. I'm pretty sure the show never actually aired.

In the wake of that, I went and paid a doctor to suck a bunch of fat out of my body. *I needed to be camera ready for the next big opportunity!*

I told myself all sorts of little lies like that in order to justify it. Really, I was tired of my trouble areas, and needed a non-vain reason to get it done. This was perfect. I could blame society and impossible television standards. It was a business move, nothing else.

The procedure went terribly. Don't ever get liposuction. A better route would be to grab a large meat tenderizer and beat the fat out of yourself. Or, you know, get on a treadmill. Either option will be fine. Another option is to just be okay with your little fat pockets that won't go away. Only the following people don't naturally have them: Olympic runners, teenage bitches (of either gender), professional ballet dancers, and for some reason monkey trainers. Everyone else has at least a handful *somewhere* on their body that they wish was gone.

Now, I don't want to disrespect all those people who have been hit by buses, so I won't use that metaphor. Instead, I will say that after the surgery it looked like I had been run over by a stagecoach. That shouldn't offend anyone. I gained 20 lbs. just from swelling. I was black and purple and weird and frumpy. Picture a giant earthworm that was recently stepped on. Repeatedly.

This lasted for about two weeks, and Noah got to see every bit of me. He was very curious about it, and I was very honest with him about what I had done.

For obvious reasons, I wanted to keep it a secret. People couldn't know that I was medically altering my body. I'm above that, don't you know. And so, I counseled heavily with five-year-old Noah that he was not to tell *anyone* under *any* circumstances.

Like the good son that he is, he promised to keep my secret.

Two days later, his mom showed up at the door to take him away. I stood as far from her as possible, draped in ultra-baggy clothing to hide the lacey pink compression suit I was being made to wear underneath (they were fresh out of the ones for guys).

She came in the house and stood in the doorway while Noah put his shoes on. "Did you have fun?" she asked him.

Without ever taking a single breath, it just began bubbling out of him, like a pot of oatmeal that you forget to keep your eye on. "Mom, guess what! Dad went to a doctor and they stuck these big sword things in him and they sucked out his fat and now he's all bloody and black and purple and swollen and super fat and he can barely walk!"

"That's the last time I tell you a secret," I grumbled.

"Sorry, Dad! I forgot I wasn't supposed to tell."

Uh huh.

Bless that kid's heart. He conveniently forgot his promise a lot. By the end of the week my sister knew. My mother knew. My best friend knew. His school teacher knew. And at least a dozen other people knew as well.

Pointless moral of the story: kids don't keep secrets, so don't share your dirt with them.

And with that, we'll get back to it...

Punch Drunk

"*Shhhh*," I hissed at Janice and Shandy who had begun giggling behind me as I worked to break into my parents' home. I knew how to finagle the back door just right to unlock it. It was a skill my brother and I acquired in all our years sneaking out of the house at night.

I held my watch up in the moonlight. 2:13 AM. Mom and Dad would not be happy if they knew I was bringing girls home from college this late.

"*Shhhh*," I hissed again. Janice and Shandy had begun their giggling anew. They didn't understand how important it was that we get in undetected.

We had planned to make it there much earlier to watch a movie in my parents' home theater, but a side trip for some skinny dipping at the hot pots down in Fillmore put us back by a few hours. As it turns out, giant and hilarious floating boobs, dancing the naked can-can, college-style truth or dare, and tip-toeing around cow pies took longer than the half hour we originally planned on.

As it was, we were now four hours from our dorm rooms at SUU, and we'd come too far to turn back.

With a solid butt bump, the door finally popped open. If we could just get inside we'd be okay. My folks never heard anything from inside. It was their thin windows to the outside that I knew were problematic. I ushered my two friends in front of me, closed the door, and we all stood inside the near pitch black theater room while our eyes adjusted.

There on the couch, so far unaware of our entrance, was Tomi Ann.

She was snoring ever so slightly. One arm was draped over the arm of the sofa, the other was wedged beneath her face. She had no pillow or blanket; observably she hadn't intended on crashing there for the night.

This wouldn't do. Not only was she occupying the space we needed to sit to watch our movie, we had brought a DVD with us that wasn't exactly up to Mom and Dad's strict standards.

In that house, there were very specific appropriate movie guidelines.

Movies could contain none of the following *really* bad words: the f-word. And I'm not talking about "fastidious" which is just fun to say. I'm talking about *the* f-word.

Also, none of the following fairly bad words: shit, bastard, bitch.

Also, none of the following not all that bad of words: damn, hell, suck.

Also, the Lord's name in vain was okay in movies, so long as it wasn't excessive, and their definition of excessive often changed depending on who was saying it and how harshly it was being said. "Oh my God" said more than twice in a row, and we could count on the movie getting turned off.

Sex in movies was a huge no-no.

Making out was a big no-no.

Even innocent kissing usually made Dad yell out, "cover your eyes!" while he reached for the remote to fast forward to a more appropriate scene. I'm 35; he still does it, though I don't watch many movies with my parents at all anymore. We just don't have the same "tastes" when it comes to blood, guts, foul language, bare bosoms, and overly entertaining hanky-panky.

Words my parents didn't forbid from movies, probably because they didn't yet know them, included: cunt, twat, and dick hole. In fact, it wouldn't be until I left the Mormon church some eleven years later that I myself learned the word *twat*. As soon as I did, I swear I heard it everywhere.

Because of their strict rules for media in their home, I knew that no amount of arguing would make them approve of our pick that night: some Adam Sandler raunchy comedy. Our movie choice was definitely the biggest reason I didn't want to wake them up. The girls and the time of night were secondary on my worry list, for sure.

And so you can see why Tomi Ann couldn't be there when we started the movie. She hadn't yet come to the dark side.

At that point in our lives, she and I had more or less stopped our bickering, and had even become friends to some degree. Moving out of the same house had been the magic pink pill that made it finally happen. Because of that, I thought maybe she would be cool enough to just scoot on down to her own bed in the basement so that we could continue our sinful evening.

I motioned my friends over toward the wall. They obliged. I went and turned on the kitchen light so that the room we were standing in wasn't so dark.

Then, I quietly knelt in front of my sister, tenderly placed one hand on her shoulder, and gave her a gentle shake. "Hey Tomi," I whispered.

She grunted and moved slightly. "Mmmm."

"I have some friends here and we want to watch a movie. Would you mind going downstairs to sleep?" I said it so quietly. So nicely. So sweetly. So…

Faster than I could process what was happening, she forcefully pushed me away from her and stood up in a fury. Her eyes shot open, heavy and bloodshot. Her nose scrunched up. Her lips pierced. And then she pulled a closed fist back, and *punched* me right in the gut. "Aaaaaah!" she literally screamed as she made impact. In my memory she sounded exactly like Miss Piggy does when she also goes on the attack.

I didn't care so much about the sucker punch. I didn't want her waking up the two people who could really put an end to our night.

"*Shhhh.* What's the matter?" I said as she wound up for punch number two. Again she swung, this time missing as I stepped out of the way.

She didn't say another word, but immediately marched out of the room and down the hallway that led to my parents' bedroom door. I sighed. So much for sliding in under the radar.

Pound. Pound. Pound. "Mom! Dad!" she screamed. "Mom! Dad!" Keep in mind, this was a grown woman, older than I.

I didn't know what to do. I thought of just ducking out the back door with my friends and disappearing, but before I could, I heard Mom's voice. "What is it?"

"Dan came home with tons of friends and he's trying to kick me out of the room!" she was screech-crying as she blurted it out.

"Dan!" Mom called me forth.

I turned to Janice and Shandy who were doing their best to blend into the wall behind them. "Shit," I murmured and I made my way toward the ridiculous mayhem unfolding.

It was dark, but I could see that Mom's door was cracked open and her head was poking out from behind. She was obviously still in her underwear and had no intentions of putting on a robe to deal with her two adult kids fighting in the middle of the night. "What's going on?" she tiredly snapped.

Tomi repeated, word for word, exactly what she had screech-cried moments earlier. "Dan came home with tons of friends and he's trying to kick me out of the room!"

I interrupted before Mom could reply. "Oh, and did she tell you that she just punched me in the stomach as hard as she could?" I demanded.

Mom gave me the same murderous look Tomi Ann had given me in the theater. "Dan, get your friends and go. You know better than to…"

I interrupted her. I honestly didn't care about Tomi Ann punching me, but I did care about the injustice of what was unfolding. "Did you hear me, Mom? Tomi Ann just punched me, and hard! I asked her nicely to..." Keep in mind, I was a grown-ass man.

Out of nowhere, Tomi Ann literally ran from the scene, crying frenziedly. She disappeared around the banister, down the basement steps, and soon her cries faded from earshot altogether.

"Mom..."

The poor woman had just been dragged out of her warm bed to the sound of her hysterical daughter pitching the world's biggest grown-up tantrum. She was beyond reason. She told me to take my friends and leave. I didn't say another word and turned to walk away. Before I took my first step, I heard Mom's door close behind me with a solid thump.

I returned to the theater and we made a dramatic exit. Once outside, I took a moment to process what had happened, and then I began laughing. I knew Tomi Ann. And yes, she could be a royal pain in my not perfect Mormon butt sometimes, but something was wrong with her that night. Something was off. That wasn't my sister.

The next time I saw her, we hugged as per the usual, and she immediately dove into a sincere and heartfelt apology for her actions the night she took a swing at her little brother. According to her, she was heavily doped on Nyquil when it all went down.

To this day, I *love* to remind her of it, and we still both laugh.

In truth, I was never angry. It would have been ridiculous to be angry. Sometimes when someone acts dramatically out of the ordinary, there's a very good bad reason for it. And they should be given a free pass.

We all do such weird and bizarre things sometimes that we normally wouldn't do. Sometimes we do destructive or vicious things and we cannot, for the lives of us, figure out why we're doing them even *as* we're doing them. Sometimes we all throw the world's biggest grown-up tantrums and then run away crying into the night.

Yes, we *all* have our moments.

Tomi Ann was punch drunk. That was her only real crime, and that's what we will always laugh at together as we reminisce back to that night.

She's also Mormon. That means she doesn't drink. But after the Nyquil incident, part of me really wants to find a way to get her completely hammered sometime and see what kind of amazing bar fight she'd start.

If that day ever happens, you better believe that only an idiot with a death wish would get involved in that.

The Mexican Kids in the Trash Pile

After I had officially flunked out of SUU, I came home to try and figure out what I was going to do with my life. I honestly had no idea *what* to do. Every female friend I had was still going to the college that had just given me the boot. All my guy friends, home and away, were now "of age." One by one they were all leaving to be Mormon missionaries for two years.

Where we lived, the population was as close to being 100% Mormon as a population could come. I'm pretty sure the only reason it wasn't 100% was because they accidentally counted the creepy Aspen tree up on Alpine Circle that looked like a guy coming at you with a Brazilian machete in the right light. The creepy murderous tree, who I shall call Kevin, was apparently *not* a Mormon, because everyone else sure was.

But, yeah. When you're a guy, and you turned 19 in Mormontowne U.S.A, you went on a mission. It's how you bring honor to your family. It's how you become worthy of your future bride. It's how you prove to the world that you weren't down at college doing the most naughty things with the most naughty girls.

I *really* didn't want to go on a mission. Trolling through strange neighborhoods for two years, knocking on the doors of strangers, and telling strict Catholics to believe in something I didn't ever believe in just didn't sound like the most appealing way to spend my time. But as all my friends disappeared, and as my 19th birthday came and went, and the pressure continued to mount, I finally consented and agreed to go. I should also mention that it didn't hurt that Mom and Dad generously offered to buy me a new car when I got back. And, no. It was not a bribe. It was a kickback from two very generous parents for giving such a big part of the best years of my life to the Lord. Okay. It was definitely kind of a bribe. And I took it.

I ended up in Mexico. The Mormon leadership doesn't give you a choice of where you'll serve. They ask God, they pick a truly inspired spot in the world, and they send you there. Or they throw darts at a map. I have no idea. All I know is that I opened "the call," it said Mexico, and that was that.

And they didn't send me to some awesome part of Mexico with white sandy beaches, or epic mariachi bands, or beautiful Latina women who desired desperately to help young gringo men acclimate by giving them shoulder rubs and potent margaritas.

No, they sent me to a part of Mexico City where you could buy ten cent tacos made from dog meat from a guy with no teeth.

And no, I'm not being facetious, nor am I making this up. Most of the meals church members served us while I was there consisted of at least one of the following... Bull testicle. Pig intestine. Chicken innards. Or on special occasions, something that vaguely resembled fish. *Every* meal was served with corn tortillas that tasted like they'd been stored on a shelf in the sewer. There were few missionaries who didn't crap their pants at least once while they were out there because of the food. I came close several times, and I promise you that had I stayed there any longer, I would have.

While I was there, which wasn't very long, I saw a man dying on the side of the road. He had been hit by a passing vehicle and left to die. Others were walking over and around him as if nothing had happened. I once watched our bus driver stop the bus, pull out a baseball bat, get out of the bus, and head toward another car. The driver of the other car pulled out a gun and our driver hurried back to his duties and drove us all away from certain murder. There was a murder-suicide right next to our apartment. A man slit his wife's throat and then his own. I was bit by a rabid dog. I was attacked with rocks and bricks by drunken gang members. I was attacked with rocks and bricks by school children. I killed a stray mutt who attacked my companion and me. I injured countless other aggressive dogs. And I saw poverty that you will never understand until you walk through it, and *live* in it.

One day in late February, Elder Petersen (my companion at the time) and I were riding the bus to go work for the day in an even poorer neighborhood on the other side of the city.

Petersen was the *perfect* Mormon missionary. Clean cut. Average build. Not too tall. Not too short. Broke no rules. Wasn't a prude. Wasn't a goof-off. Woke up on time every morning. Prayed for an hour every night. Only shit his pants once while we were serving together. He made me work, which was annoying, but he didn't ever act like he was better than me, which was rare.

While on the bus that day, we passed a *huge* mountain of garbage that had collected in an abandoned lot between two cinderblock shacks. It must have been fifteen feet high at least. Trash was nothing new for us. Entire streets were used for dumping trash. It was everywhere.

But on this particular trash heap, nine or ten kids were scattered across it, rummaging for whatever it is poverty-stricken Mexican kids rummage. If I had to guess, most of them fell between the ages of four and seven. Most of them were without shoes. Most of them were emaciated and filthy. Most of them wore tattered rags for clothes.

And I, the all-important, well-fed, giant white man began making fun of them in English to my companion.

I made fun of them.

I laughed at them.

I don't remember what I said, but I remember kind of what I said, and I remember the taunting and jeering tone I said it in.

"Ooooh, look Paquito, I found me a piece of a poop-covered shoe! Maybe I'll boil it and eat it for dinner tonight!" Something ass-holish like that.

I expected my companion to laugh at my amazing humor.

Instead, he became infuriated and chewed my ass out without holding anything back.

"Elder Pearce, you do not ever, in front of me, make fun of these people again. *Ever.* You do not know what kind of lives they have lived that brought them to that trash pile. You do not know what they have been through just to survive. You do not know where their parents are, or if they're even alive. You do not know where they go at night when they need to sleep. You don't know *anything* about those kids. And I promise you, if you…"

"Okay, okay, geez," I said, cutting him off. And I slunk deep into my seat.

I couldn't make eye contact with him for the rest of the day. I don't think we said more than two words to each other the entire trip home.

I could use a cliché and say that I felt like a tiny nothing in that moment, but I won't. I very much felt like a big something. A big ass. I wanted to wither away and disappear. I was so tied into my first world life and my first world problems, that I could not look at innocent children rummaging through garbage for their own survival and feel even the slightest bit of compassion. Not before he lambasted me the way he did.

And I don't think I had ever been as thankful for any lesson as I was for that one, that day on the bus. In one twenty second diatribe, a friend shook me enough to teach me compassion for others. He loved me enough to silence my idiocy. For good.

As I think back to that trash pile, and those tiny children rummaging through it, I can't help but think how the further I get away from it, the easier it becomes to not care anymore. The more time dims that memory, the more I forget that there is real struggling and real poverty in this world.

And even worse, I forget how much I *have*. I forget how blessed I truly am. I begin focusing on what I want and what I *don't* have instead. I forget that I'm just another all-important, well fed, giant white man.

And it was luck only that made me that. I chose to be born in the place, time, and family I was born into as much as those Mexican children chose to be born into theirs, and just as much as someone chose to be born into the ghetto, or China, or in some bathroom at Denny's.

Which is to say, I didn't choose it at all, neither did you, and neither did anyone else.

So how can I ever be so underdeveloped, and so ignorant, as to forget that?

I truly believe that laughing at inappropriate things is an essential skill that we must all learn.

But what I said as we passed the garbage pile that day was a true sign of my immaturity. It was a sign of doucheyness. It was a sign of the sense of entitlement I so obviously carried. There was nothing funny about it.

I have come to believe that in such moments is where we begin to differentiate ourselves as wise or foolish people. When we learn the difference between the inappropriate things we *can* laugh at, and what ultimately should be off limits, we become *better* people.

And I hope for the rest of my life, my friends will care about me as much as my companion did, and fiercely call me out on it should I ever slip into such thinking or entitled jeering again.

The Baseball Bat

What Petersen had said to me as we passed the garbage pile was still nibbling away at my insides as I sat wedged between him and twelve other Mexicans in the back of a combi some two weeks later. Combi was what the Chilangos called the Volkswagen vans that acted as unofficial taxis in the big city. The fare was cheap thanks to their broad willingness to forgo any and all personal space. The most people I'd ever seen crammed into the back of one was 18.

The woman straight across from me was holding two chickens on her lap. She had tied ropes around their necks like little leashes. I'd seen plenty of dog meat for sale, it would only make sense that these chickens were family pets.

The smell of hard and constant booze poured off the man next to me who was looking straight forward with glossed and bloodshot eyes. I couldn't tell if he was awake, asleep, or dead. Maybe a combination of all three.

None of these people had bathed in days, maybe weeks. Maybe years. A small girl sat on her father's lap staring at me with her giant black eyes. She'd probably never seen a 6'4" giant white man with blonde hair and blue eyes before. Most Mexicans stared at me.

Still, as much as I hated being a missionary, and as much as I didn't believe in what I was doing as a Mormon missionary, I was really beginning to like Mexico City.

To some degree it was exciting, knowing that I was flirting with death in everything I did down there. One wrong turn and I would get shot, stabbed, or eaten by those damned wild dogs. One sip of the wrong water or bite of underprepared food, and I'd be shitting my own organs out.

As I fought to stay awake in the combi, my mind drifted again to those kids rummaging through the garbage. As much as I hated hearing it, what Petersen had said to me was a crucial wake-up call. He was right. I was turning into a prick.

My companion poked me in the shoulder. At some point I had drifted off. "Our stop's coming up." He yelled for the driver to pull-over, passed him thirty pesos, and we finagled our way through the other passengers until we were more or less pushed out the door. We had probably hoofed it at least 16 miles on foot that day already. Another half mile and we'd be home for the evening.

From seemingly nowhere, an intense stabbing pain shot from my hip down into my leg. *What the crap was that?* I took another step. The same debilitating pain shot down my leg again. "Petersen, stop. Something's wrong. I can't walk," I said.

I attempted a few more steps and found myself completely handicapped and unable to continue.

Two weeks later I stepped off of a plane in California. When my hip went bad I was thrilled. I mean, I was *certain* it was my ticket home. Instead they transferred me to Riverside where I'd be given the use of a car to continue God's work. The orthopedic surgeon in Mexico assured everyone involved that less walking would most likely make the problem go away. Unfortunately, he was right, and in little time at all, the pain in my hip went away completely.

For the next five months, I tried to make it as a missionary. I really did.

I tried to have a good attitude. I tried not to hate it. I tried to actually believe what I was preaching door to door. Each day I told people that if they would simply read a few chapters of my church's scripture, and then pray to know whether or not it was true, they'd receive an answer that it most definitely was. Each day, I myself read *several* chapters of scripture and prayed about it, but never got any such answer. Ever. *You're lying to these people. You shouldn't be here. You don't belong out here,* I often thought.

But I couldn't go home. Missionaries who went home early and without a damn good reason were considered weak. They were quitters. Their morals and their worthiness was questioned. My family would ostracize me. My community would coldshoulder me. No Mormon girl would ever want me. I was completely certain of all those things.

But… you're lying to people. You're promising something that you can't even make happen for yourself.

Maybe I was. Maybe I was confused. Maybe I was just young and stupid. I do know that I never truly believed in the religion at all, and trying to force myself to do so wasn't working. At least if I was at home I could fake it. At home I didn't have to live it, breathe it, and share it all day every day. At home I could pretend to be a good believing member of the church. But out on the streets with a suit and a nametag… I hated it.

The majority of my Mormon mission, of which I completed 43% before finding a way to get out of it, can be summed up very quickly.

Blisters. Masturbation. Parasites. Diarrhea. Dead hobos. Inbred housemates. Hypersexualized 13-year-old girls. Slutty missionary companions having sexual encounters with those hypersexualized 13-year-old-girls. Slutty younger women. Slutty older women. More diarrhea. Doodles of naked women. Doodles of naked men. Masturbation. Rabies. Rabies shots. Rumors of gay missionaries. Heavy weight loss. Heavy weight gain. Sneaking onto golf courses. Murderous drunks. Sleep walking. Shitting in holes in the ground. Drug dealers threatening to end my fat white man life if I ever bring my little white man dick up in here again. Children sucker punching me in the junk. White trash women purposefully giving me glimpses of their entire bare breasts just to tease me while their shit-faced boyfriends laughed about it. And, oh yeah. Taking a baseball bat to my own spine to finally get away from it all. I guess I can't leave that one off the list.

Eventually I was at the point on my mission where I *needed* an out. I needed to go home. I needed to find a way to be granted an honorable discharge; a get out of jail free card, if you will. I needed people to think that I wasn't a quitter. I needed people to think that I wasn't a loser. I had had enough rejection. Classmates. Girls. Missionaries. God Himself. Not to mention all the people behind all the many doors that were slammed in my face every day.

I can promise you that you never feel like a bigger schmuck than when you're knocking on doors in 120-degree heat, and an *old* lady in a floral shower cap tells you to go stick your dicks into each other and leave her the hell alone.

Unfortunately for me, it seemed that the only early releases that people back home thought honorable were for medical reasons or a death in the immediate family. Nobody in my family had a foot in the grave, and with my hip no longer giving me troubles, I was drawing blanks.

It was at breakfast one morning that I took special notice of the metal baseball bat leaning against the doorframe of my bedroom entryway. The mental cogs immediately started turning as I sat with a mouthful of Frosted Flakes. *That's it. That's my ticket out of this place.*

It was a ludicrous idea. It was not lost on me that I was *officially* crazy. But I was going to do it anyway. I couldn't stand to look one more stranger in the face as a missionary.

My companion finished his own breakfast. He'd go shower now. He always got ready for the day after he finished his corn flakes. And... right on cue. "I'm going to go shower," he said. I told him to take his time.

As soon as I heard the water running and the shower curtain close, I walked over and picked up the baseball bat. I slid it back and forth through my open palm. *Don't do it.* I was going to do it. *Don't do it.* I needed to do it. It was the only way.

I carried the bat into my bedroom and shut the door behind me. I positioned myself face-down on the carpet and lifted the bat as high as I could above me. It was definitely awkward in this position. *Just enough to hurt yourself.* With a heavy swing I made impact on my lower spine. *Crap, that hurt.* It wasn't enough. I did it again. Still not enough. *Do you realize how crazy this is?* I hit myself again, much harder this time. *I don't care. I need to get out of here.*

It took more than fifty hits with the bat to cripple myself, and just in time, too. The water in the bathroom stopped running, and I hurried and shoved the bat across the floor and under my bed. Within minutes the bedroom door opened and my companion stood in the doorway looking down at me. "What are you doing?"

"Something's seriously wrong with my back. I can't move. I can't walk. We're going to have to cancel our appointments today," I moaned.

A couple weeks later, I was stepping off another plane, this time into the arms and embraces of my immediate and extended family. I had been given a medical discharge. An *honorable* discharge.

I limped as I walked, nursing the sudden back injury that medicine couldn't explain. The doctors had recommended I use a cane until my back healed. Instead, I opted to walk with the assistance of one very special metal baseball bat.

I buried this memory as quickly as I could and I kept it buried for many years. I never made mention of it until I wrote about it in my *Bullied: The Forgotten Memoirs.* series on my blog, which few people ever read due to its depressing nature and overwhelming length.

A reporter for The New York Times flew out to interview me shortly after I shared it and asked if it was true. Of all the stories he had heard and read about me, he was hung up on this one the most. When he interviewed my ex-wife, he was more curious about her knowledge of this story than anything else. Had I told her about it? Had I ever mentioned it at all? Was I making it up to get blog traffic or attention? Why had I never told *anyone* about crippling myself with the baseball bat, including her?

The reason was simple enough. It was the craziest thing I had ever done in my life. And I don't use the word *crazy* lightly. I had to be mentally ill to take a bat to my own spine, or at the very least I had to be temporarily insane. And, you know what? It's embarrassing to be crazy.

As I wrote that story out, and for the first time really *thought* about what it all meant, what it pointed to, and what lessons were learned, I was sad that I buried that secret for so long. In truth, it wasn't actually crazy or insane. It wasn't even embarrassing. It was the very real truth of what a high-pressure society and subculture will do to otherwise normal people.

I learned that people will do drastic things to escape the corners we paint them into.

People *long* for happiness. We all do. It's the one thing we strive for most during our short time on this Earth. They also strive for authenticity. The further we get into life, and the closer we get to death, the more unsatisfied we become living lives that other people order and push us into.

I don't know why we believe we can dictate to others how they should be living their lives, what they should be believing, and defining all that is so black and white.

When we put heavy pressure on others to do what *we* think is right because we are afraid of how their actions will reflect on *us*, we will often push them into extremely dangerous circumstances.

And who wants that? I sure don't. I'd rather you push me into a giant bowl of Crème Brule instead. At least getting myself out of that sticky mess would be a delight.

The Potato Cannon

The year I temporarily crippled myself with the baseball bat was a year of boner moves all around. I'm talking real Darwin Award stuff.

A college buddy and I had figured out from ye glorious Internet how to build potato cannons, and we went all-out building full-on six-foot long bazookas. We spent many hours having spectacular amounts of fun shooting potatoes 300-500 feet into the mountains. I think it was only natural for me to want to share some of this goodness with my other, much crazier pals.

Enter Spencer.

He was in our group of boner friends, and we all did a *lot* of boner things together.

We used to kick each other in the groins. For fun. Explain that one to me.

We used to pin each other down, dig our hands as far into each other's butt holes as possible, and yell G.O.T.D. (it stood for gay of the day) as loud as we could while burrowing as deep as we could. For fun. Explain that one to me, too.

Other times we'd grab old ratty bath towels, roll them just so, tie rubber bands around the ends, wet the tips, and run around like hooligans whipping each other. For fun. We called them rat tail wars. Blood was drawn many times.

Bloody knuckles. Slaps. Licorice whipping. Mattress wars. Fun. Fun. Fun. Fun.

One of our favorite games was "dodge the paintball" in which we'd stand one at a time, 20 feet in front of a firing squad, and we didn't get to "move out" until we could successfully dodge a surprise ball of paint hurling our way at 178 MPH. For fun. It usually took several attempts and a whole lot of welts for me to dodge one, but it was all worth it because then it was my turn to inflict some pain on the others.

We loved that game, so of *course* it led to me and Spencer creating a cross-over version of it using my new potato cannon. We plotted it out with no thought at all, and called our new game "Dodge the Potato."

In case you're not aware of what a potato cannon is, let me fill you in.

A potato cannon (or spud gun) is a homemade firearm, usually created with PVC piping, a barbecue igniter, and other fun stuff. It's a simple contraption. You stuff a potato down the barrel of your cannon with a broomstick, then you pour or spray some sort of explosive into the other end, and then... you ignite it.

Did I mention that the potato often launches more than 300 feet? The furthest launch I've seen was about 500 feet, though that's just a guestimate since it completely disappeared from our view. In other words, these things are powerful and you should never, ever, ever, *ever* shoot one at another person.

But, twenty-year-olds don't think that way. In fact, call me crazy but twenty-year olds think they're bulletproof and incapable of any actual or long-term harm. We took it one step further, believing we were potato proof, as well.

Now, these homemade cannons are often finicky. It sometimes takes several attempts to get them to shoot, let alone to get them to shoot accurately. So, we made a rule. We'd each take a turn shooting potatoes at each other, and our turn would end either when we hit the other person or after six failed attempts to do so.

Spencer lost the paper, rock, scissors and had to go first. I started with three misfires and no successful potatoes launched. My fourth shot did launch, but it skipped along the ground twenty feet or so to

Spencer's left. Shots #5 and #6 were also misfires, so I handed the cannon over to Spencer, confident that I would be just as fortunate as he was, bummed that I hadn't nailed my friend with a big ass potato.

I jogged 70 feet or so into the field, the distance we decided together was safe. I stood there like an idiot, watching him spray WD-40 into the chamber, jam a potato deep inside, and grin like a sadist clown while he did it.

He picked up the cannon and swung it in my direction. As I stared into its dark barrel, I couldn't help but start wondering how good an idea this actually was. I squatted in my "dodge it" position, and waited for a possible potato headed my way.

And... *shoooonk.* The gun went off. On his *first damn shot.*

I can still see the potato heading toward me in slow motion.

I jumped to the left in my attempt to dodge it, and as if the potato had heat seeking capabilities, it followed me.

The whole thing happened in less than the snap of a finger, but slow enough that I could process it all happening as it did. It was headed straight for my abdomen. I instinctively lifted my hand to block the potato, but the spud was too fast. My hand got there right after the potato made impact, which was probably a blessing because it likely would have shattered the bones in my hand.

I caught the raw potato in my hand, or at least a few pieces of it. The potato had hit my pudgy gut so hard that it burst into ten or so different pieces, most of which somehow ended up inside of my sweatshirt pocket.

I instantly was blown backwards, or I fell backwards (I'm not sure which), very much aware that I was about to die. I was prostrate in the field, attempting to grasp what had just happened, trying to find the ability to breathe. No breath came for quite some time. If I could sum up how it felt, I'd say it was akin to having a gorilla jump up and down on my stomach as I lay helpless among the awful stickers and sage brush.

Spencer set the cannon down and started sprinting across the field, in riots.

I still was struggling to get a full breath in.

Then I realized that I had no feeling in my legs. And I mean *no* feeling. This awareness made me even more desperate to breathe.

He got to where I was sprawled out and dying, and continued his horrible laughing charge. "First try!" he exclaimed, far too proud of himself, and completely oblivious to the fact that I hadn't yet inhaled.

Somewhere in the middle of his glee, I finally was able to suck in a small amount of wind. It was painful, but it was enough to keep me alive. "Dude, something's wrong." He was laughing too hard to hear me. I just lay there, barely breathing, grimacing, fighting back the urge to cry. Willing my toes to wiggle.

It was probably more than a minute until I felt sensation start to enter my lower extremities again.

That was an entire minute that I was *sure* I was going to be paralyzed for life, and let me tell you that the seconds don't click by very fast when you're thinking thoughts of wheelchairs and pressure sores.

Within a few minutes I was able to walk. A few minutes after that the pain had mostly subsided and I just felt a dull ache where the tuber had hit me.

"I don't think this was the best idea," I said, now laughing at what a completely ridiculous game it had ended up being. Spencer agreed, but only because he didn't want to be standing back out in that field getting a potato in his own gut.

Out of curiosity, we loaded the cannon once more. I wanted to see the close-range power of it. We stood ten feet from a fire hydrant and let 'er rip. *Shoooonk.* Nothing was left of the potato but a wet spot where it made impact.

Spencer and I both looked at the splotch on the fire hydrant and then at each other. "We're idiots," I told him. With wide eyes, he nodded in agreement.

I never fired that potato cannon again.

It seems silly to say, "I learned something from that." I mean, of *course* I learned something from the potato cannon incident. I learned that friends shouldn't shoot each other with potatoes.

But I learned something else much more important, too. I learned that when we let pride trap us into stupid situations, we *always* still have a choice to walk away.

As I looked into the barrel of that cannon, I *knew* it was a bad idea. I *knew* I might get really hurt in the moments that followed. But my pride and my testosterone got in the way of me saying, "sorry bro, I'm not going to do this." I didn't want to seem like the pussy. I didn't want to disrespect the way we, as a group of friends, always followed through on our own painful side of the sadomasochistic games we so often played. And I really didn't want to be laughed at by the others in our bigger group for my cowardice.

Spencer also experienced the same thing I had out in that field. That dude had a third degree black belt, could do backflips, and looked like an underwear model. And still, he told me later that he also realized how stupid an idea it was the moment I swung the cannon in his direction.

I learned that only the bravest people will let themselves be thought weaklings in such moments.

We *all* find ourselves in self-arrived situations that are stupid or reckless or just plain bad for us from time to time, and as I've watched people over the years, I've learned that very few people walk away from them, almost always because of pride or testosterone. And in every situation, they could have.

Now I try to recognize those situations, and I try to walk away from them. And yes, it's usually to the taunting jeers of the people I'm with, but at least I don't find myself flattened on my back at the foot of a mountain, wondering if I'll be able to find my next breath.

Mom. Grandma.

After returning from the mission, I lived with my parents just long enough for two things to occur. I was almost manslaughtered by that flying spud; and I was almost murdered by my mother. Both of these events happened within an approximate one-week time span.

It was no secret in our household that I butted heads *big time* with Mom and Dad, particularly in the latter half of my upbringing. I'd like to say I didn't carry disdain for them when I was going through the ages of hurting preteen to asshole teenager and all the way to vexed full-grown man, but I can't do so honestly. I was (more often than not) overly resentful of them, bitter, and angry for the ways they parented. I'd even go so far as to say that I generally loathed them both.

But they shouldn't take that too personally. After all, two things are true.

First, I seemingly loathed everyone and everything back then. I loathed brushing my teeth. I loathed Barry Manilow. I loathed mushrooms and beets. And as far as I know, Barry Manilow didn't take it personally, and neither did the mushrooms. Therefore, neither should my parents. That's sound logic, right?

Second, Mom and Dad carried plenty of disdain for *me*. Oh, I'm sure they'd tell me they didn't. No *real* parents loathe their own kids, after all. But oh, how it seemed to me that I was loathed by my two creators. And, how could they *not* feel any other way? I was a relentless weenie to them. I made their lives as miserable as I possibly could.

They had really damn good reasons to detest me just as so many parents around the world have damn good reasons to detest their own belligerent and limit-pushing adolescents.

Teenagers are just assholes sometimes.

And so are parents. It's inevitable.

I mean, think about it. Teenage boys are going through this weird part of life where the following is almost always true.

They are thinking mostly with their penises, but they don't yet know much about their penises, how to use them effectively, or when they should be using them at all. Their brains are not fully developed. They're literally still missing those developed parts of the brain that think erudite things such as, "dude, you probably shouldn't ride on top of a speeding car naked," or "dude, you should probably go to class instead of to your girlfriend's dorm room."

Teenagers are too old to be coddled and too young to be given free reign of their own lives. They want Mom and Dad to still supply *everything* and they don't want Mom and Dad to have a say in *anything*.

It's a seriously tough place to be for most teenagers.

And parents, well, they're not in any easier of a place in life. I'm guessing that the following is almost always true.

When thinking through how to handle their teenagers, parents obviously don't do it in the same way their kids do. They don't do so with their sex organs, and they also don't do so with the stupid parts of their brains. Those undeveloped areas of their minds that could very much help parents empathize and understand the way their teenagers think literally doesn't exist for them anymore.

So, they attempt to parent while thinking with their developed minds and with their hearts the way real adults do. That is dangerous, I know. I mean, their brains are actually thinking smart things like, "give him his space," or "establish your authority and don't budge. It will be good for him in the long run."

But when they do that, undeveloped-dum-dum-brain-teens see that space as avoidance and distrust, and they see their parents' authority and unwillingness to budge as methodical oppression. It's a no-win situation for everyone, at least when the teenager is as oppositionally defiant as I was.

And those poor, poor parents. Their minds and their hearts never let up, and are often in such extreme conflict with one another. The older their teenagers get, the more parents must choose which of their two thinking organs they will let dictate their own parenting actions. Their minds tell them to cut their kids loose, let them fly and fall on their own, and to give their kids more freedom over their own lives so that they can one day be responsible adults. Their hearts tell them to hold on longer, control their kids' lives as much as possible so that they don't make all those unnecessary mistakes, and to continue to both coddle and supply their kids with what they need for as long as they need it.

Teenager brains are always developing. Always changing. Sometimes evolving. Sometimes regressing.

Parent brains are doing the exact same thing.

And the cogs eventually stop lining up between parent and teenager. Slightly at first, then one day entirely. The inner-workings of the parent-child relationships get clogged and jammed. And the parents begin to loathe their teenagers and the teenagers begin to loathe their parents. And eventually it *all* erupts. Somebody snaps. And an adult is *finally* born out of all of it.

It was at this point in which Mom and I found ourselves that one fateful week, not long after I returned from the mission. We were at our eruption point. One of us was bound to go off.

In exchange for letting me live with them, and in exchange for all of my food, and utilities, and general financial support, Mom and Dad asked only one thing of me. Wash the dishes every night. The terms were easy enough to agree with at the time I made the deal.

But I started up at the local community college that same week. I wanted girls in my life. I wanted to spend time with my friends. I wanted to go shoot potatoes at Spencer. I wanted to write a novel. I definitely wanted to ejaculate as often as possible. Don't get me wrong. I had good intentions to wash those dishes, and most of the time I kept my commitment, but I wasn't perfect at it.

And one night, after a big messy meal, I didn't do them.

I promised Mom it'd be done in the morning first thing. She very reluctantly agreed.

I didn't do them the next morning, either.

And, she erupted.

I'm not saying she simply started yelling, or huffing, or puffing, or any of that mild stuff that I was so used to. I'm saying, she *erupted*.

The culmination of our years butting heads together all came to one glorious point, and I watched mesmerized as she literally jumped up and down, stamped her feet, waved her arms, and began *screaming* at the top of her lungs. She was having a full on tantrum.

I don't remember what she was screaming, but I remember these three phrases at the end, each screamed as loud and as high as her windpipe could make them while she jumped up and down in front of me.

"Get out!"

"Get out!"

"GET OOOOUUUUUT!"

It was the first and only time since I was a child that I remember being sincerely *scared* of my mother. If she would have had a weapon that could inflict blunt force trauma in that moment, some uncontrolled part of her *might* have used it. Have no doubt.

When she finally finished, she just stood, looking at me with terrified and angry eyes.

Those eyes.

I can never forget what they told me in that moment. They said, "I don't know *what* the hell that was that just came out of me," and "you better get out of my sight before it happens again." It was like standing in front of a big purple Tyrannosaurus Rex who doesn't understand why he suddenly isn't singing "I Love You" and dancing with children, but instead is desperately desiring to rip those children limb to limb.

Not wanting to be dismembered, I obeyed her eyes, and I disappeared into my bedroom down in the basement.

Before I could even sit on my bed and attempt to process what had just happened, the intercom cracked throughout the entire house. "Dan, you need to find yourself a new place to live. Today." It clicked and went silent.

I immediately packed two large duffel bags and within twenty minutes I was back at the top of the stairs. It was time to be on my own. I knew it. She knew it.

And in that moment, an adult was born.

She was standing in the upstairs hallway as I pushed my way past her, carrying my bags. She tried to apologize, I ignored her. She tried again. I ignored her again. She tried once more, I turned to her and with an ice-cold tone, told her that she didn't need to worry. I would never live in her house again.

That was fourteen years ago. My brain has since more fully developed, and I've actually learned how to use it. I follow my gut more often than I don't. My penis has finally taken a back seat to my heart. *Most* of the decisions I make nowadays are sound.

I also have a child of my own, which will do more to help any person understand his own parents and the way they raised him than any amount of therapy could ever offer.

And I watch him with her sometimes.

My son is eight right now. He *loves* his Nana.

I watch Nana. She *loves* her grandson.

I watch the two of them play, and laugh, and hug, and wrestle, and interact. There is only kindness and goodness there. I watch her when she needs to use her authority with him. There is only sweetness, albeit firm sweetness, there as well.

Meh. That's just how grandparenting is. Believe me, I've thought the thought myself. But there is more to it than that, and this is where I have really learned a lesson when it comes to my mother.

You see, now that my brain is working a little better, I have an important ability. I have the ability to zoom out from any situation. It's an ability that teenagers generally lack. And when I zoom out from what Mom and I had together, I am able to put a lot of things into perspective that I never could when I was younger.

For much of my adult life, I remembered Mom as a tyrant. I remembered her as always angry. Always upset. Always demanding. Never forgiving. Never budging. Always over-bearing. Far too strict. Overly mean. And I was convinced she had it out for her kids.

As I aged, I eventually zoomed out enough to realize that *all* of that was me and her and it certainly wasn't all the time, or even most of the time. My siblings have nowhere close to the same memory of my parents that I do. They generally remember her as supportive. And kind. And fun. And silly. And strong. And encouraging. And yes, strict, but not unreasonably.

At first, it hurt when I realized this. Sure, I had always thought myself the black sheep of the family, but I never had thought I was the *only* one who was loathed or despised or (was it possible?) even hated by my parents.

But over time I learned something and I eventually replaced that hurt with the truth.

Sometimes two people's personalities just *clash*.

I am a kind, loving, silly, fun, awesome person. To *almost* everyone. But there are a few people in this world who have never really wronged me, and I have never really wronged them, yet we cannot *stomach* being around one another. Just being in the same room is difficult for everyone as the tension becomes so thick and ugly that a professional lumberjack couldn't chop through it.

I *hate* the person that I become when these people are around. I *hate* that I can't seem to control it, and I *hate* that I seem to become a different person any time they are near. I *hate* that I *loathe* them as much as I do.

I'd love to change all of that, but for some reason I *can't*. Our clashing personalities simply won't allow it, so the best we can find to do is pretend the other doesn't exist, even when we're standing right next to one another.

And this is what I've learned when it comes to these people, and more importantly to my mother.

I've learned that sometimes every one of us simply won't mesh with another person, but that doesn't mean that *our* perception of that person is a fair one or an accurate one.

Who *I* saw my mother as is not who my mother actually is. It's just who she was with me, and I was half to blame for that. Who my mother saw me as, and who I actually am, also differed completely.

Our personalities just crashed together in horrible ways. It's as simple and as difficult an idea as that.

Where I got lucky was that we both eventually learned how to zoom out and see who the other was without our own ugly filters blinding us to the truth. We've both learned that we aren't who we always thought we were when we ourselves are not in the picture. Our respect for each other has become sincere. Our friendship has grown. Our hugs have become genuine. It just took some growing-up to get to that point.

Indeed, this was the greatest lesson of all. I have learned from my relationship with Mom now, and our relationship then, that I cannot judge *anyone* fairly unless I am able to extract myself from the equation completely and actually *see* who they are when they are with everyone else.

After doing that, I have to admit. Mom is a pretty damn awesome lady, who has far more goodness in her than she has demons, and it has become nearly impossible to see her as anything other than a love-filled, passionate, embracing, and selfless woman.

"O.L."

It will be difficult for me to ever forget the day I stepped onto ye glorious bathroom scale and instead of a number, it simply read, "OL."

What OL meant, I didn't know. I do know that it appeared when I finally tipped the scales at 350 lbs.

Did it mean over the limit? Over-load? Out of luck? OFF LARD-ASS!

Three and a half bills.

Three hundred and fifty pounds.

I weighed so much that even my high-capacity scale was being a jerk to me about it.

Up until that moment, I had always been able to rationalize my fatness.

There wasn't much I could do about it.

My family had terrible fat genes. Just about everyone in my entire family and in my extended family fell somewhere between chubby and manatee. This included the ones who had run marathons in the past and who had lived the occasional lifestyle of steadfast fitness. Yes, it was my genes. It had to be. And the proof was there, so long as I didn't count Eric, who had always been so annoyingly fit and skinny. Or those one cousins who somehow had missed the bad gene memo.

I also was trapped in a society that gave me no choice but to be fat. It wasn't my fault they had fast food on every corner. Nor was it my fault that technology had pushed my generation into sedentary sit-around all day jobs. And let's not forget that with the day and age we live in, people just have to work 60-80 hours a week to even make it anymore. There was no time for exercise, and the proof was there. So long as I conveniently never noticed my still very fit office chums or the healthier choices that were being offered at these fast food restaurants I liked to frequent.

Between the fat genes theory and society, I had my own guilt taken care of.

Plus, *everyone* likes big jolly fat guys, so why change? We're the life of the party. We are the funniest ones in the room. We are sweet and good for empathetic hugs and funny dancing.

"OL."

I stood on the scale that day and stared at it for a good two minutes. I didn't like those two giant ugly letters staring back at me.

Maybe it was a glitch. I stepped off and back on again. "OL."

I stepped off again and this time just put one foot on the scale. 57 lbs. *It's working. Damn it.*

I suddenly felt the weight of my bad health decisions like never before. Strangely, no pun intended.

I didn't know how I got to 350 lbs. I never had to know because no one ever has to know how they get there. The road to morbid obesity is paved with hundreds of diets and thousands of good intentions. The formula for life-threatening corpulence compounds with just one poor decision and one extra pound at a time. One bad decision at a time. And I know from doing it that it's incredibly easy to rationalize that one extra pound or that one bad decision, *every single time.* The easiest and truest words quite possibly may be, "well, one pound is easy enough to take off. No big deal."

I really believe that I lost *thousands* of pounds to finally push the scale so far into the ground that it groaned. I was the champion of weight loss. I was the fount of all exercise and fitness knowledge.

Fat people usually are.

I promise you, few groups of people on this earth have studied health and fitness the way fat people have. Few groups of people have studied exercise and diet the way fat people have. Few groups of people know more about what it takes to be healthy or to lose weight than all the fat people have.

If you want to know how to be in the best shape and best health of your life, go ask a really fat person how to do it, and *do* what they tell you to do.

Don't ask a skinny person who has never known what it is like to publicly declare that Old Navy must have changed the way they size their clothes because you *know* you haven't gained two inches since the last time you went in. Skinny people don't know much about it at all. It's like asking a coal miner how to sky dive. You just don't do that.

Fat people have read all the break-through books about diet and weight-loss. They've tried the programs. They've joined groups and classes at their gyms. And, they've been successful more times than you can imagine. They have watched the scale drop, and they've watched it drop big time. Many times. They have watched the stack of weights increase at the gym. Many times. I'm telling you, they know what they're doing.

Just don't ask them how to change their lives perpetually. That's where fat people are lost. You see, fat people (and I can say this because I was a *really* fat guy) attack their weight. Which is where they go wrong every time.

All that extra weight… it's really not the problem. It's a *symptom* of the problem, and fat people usually don't understand that. They believe that all of their problems (or at least most of them) will go away if they can just get skinny. But in reality, it's the other way around. All of the fat will go away (or at least most of it) if they can just get to the root of their *problems* and if they can just get to the root of *why* they let themselves get fat in the first place, and *why* they continually grease their arteries, and *why* they slowly kill themselves with hamburgers, soda, and potato chips.

"OL." I didn't know what it stood for. But I suddenly understood that I had to learn why I had let myself get to that point. Why had I rationalized it for so long? Why did I not care enough about myself to be healthy? Why had I been strangely okay becoming even more of the very thing I loathed most about myself? What was the root of all of it? Why was I eating toward my earlier death?

Weighing nearly a sixth of a ton was not exactly a walk in the park. It was more like a moment in the park where you're bent over in agony because the first block you just jogged gave you such a bad side-cramp that you legitimately fear your organs are about to start failing you.

This is what life was like for me, weighing more than a fully-loaded refrigerator:

I would wake up in a panic at night thinking that someone had dropped a golf ball into my throat any time my neck fat suddenly clamped off my trachea. I had large, beautiful (*all natural, baby!*) breasts. I didn't fit inside the seats on the old White Rollercoaster as was so graciously pointed out to me by the pimple-faced attendant. I could *make* myself fit inside trendy clothing that was two sizes too small for me. There were ways to believe that donuts were healthy sometimes. My penis literally would suck up inside of me when I sat down and bent over in a cold room. And, I made most skinny people nervous. Especially buffet managers and Geek Squad employees.

When the scale read back "OL," something triggered inside of me. I knew what I had to do. I knew what I needed to do. And, I knew what I wanted to do. My lifestyle had to change. Permanently.

So, I did the next best thing to actually fixing myself, and the next best thing to getting to the roots of my problems, and I had a surgeon cut my innards up into little pieces. One year later, I weighed 192 lbs.

That was when the doctor told me that I would die if I didn't find a way to put back on another thirty pounds. My hip bones were protuberant. My rib cage was visible and defined. My tailbone was protruding. I reminded myself of this particular feral dog down in Mexico who was missing most of his tail. That dog tried to kill me, but thankfully it was so emaciated and weak that a solid kick from my Dr. Marten boot punctured its rib cage and he left me alone as he skulked away to die.

And here, at the skinniest I had ever been since I was eight years old, a doctor was telling me to *gain* weight or die. My tailbone was grinding into everything causing me infection after infection. I eventually developed an allergy to penicillin and, as the doctor so eloquently put it, eventually I'd become allergic to all the antibiotics and there would be nothing they could do to fend off the infections anymore. I needed some blubber on my butt.

This is what life was like for me, as a way too skinny person:

Skiing became fun instead of terrifying. I could run without cramping up. I could shop for clothes at places that *weren't* Old Navy. I bruised easily and all the time. I developed giant abscesses near my tailbone that had to be painfully lanced. My beautiful breasts disappeared. People complimented me. A lot. Especially fat people. My boners were suddenly *huge*. I made most fat people nervous. And, buffet managers loved me because I didn't eat much of anything and my tables were always freed up sooner than later. I still made Geek Squad employees nervous. I guess they don't like tall people, either.

I think the most fun I've ever had in my life was during that six months when I was *trying* to gain 30 lbs. so that I "wouldn't die."

You know how donuts are just about the best thing ever? Maple bars, specifically?

Well, try eating a doctor-ordered Maple Bar. It's like having a doctor tell you to introduce crack into your diet. It's wonderful. And magical. And so much fun.

Until you realize you can't do it anymore. Then it becomes almost impossible to stop.

After I had gained my thirty pounds and within no time at all, I found myself doing the exact things I had always done which had pushed me to that fateful day when the scale read "OL." Yo-yo diets. Rationalization. Blaming the family genes. And at 250 lbs, I saw what I was doing, and I *knew* that if I didn't solve what had made me fat in the first place, that scale would one day read "OL" again.

The day the numbers on the scale read 250, I dedicated myself to *fixing* myself. I promised myself I would get rid of every ghost and every demon that I was perceptibly carrying around with me.

That was nine years ago. I have kept that promise ever since. And I've learned something as I've kept my promise.

Overcoming those ghosts and demons from my past is *much* harder than losing weight on crash diets and whatever latest pill hits the market.

It involves a lot of trial and error. It involves therapy. It involves righting past wrongs. It involves letting go of past anger, resentment, and hatred. It involves finally facing things that have been buried or left in the past.

More than anything, it involves journaling. Journaling has a way of accomplishing most or all of that. It gives me therapy. After all, most therapy is simply a person sitting in a chair while you sort out your own feelings to them. Journaling helps you know what you are holding onto and who you resent. It helps you deal with the things that give you anger and hatred. It gives you a place to confront those ghosts and demons from your past.

For me, my journal was public. Several years into my goal of fixing myself, I did it in the form of a blog. I never intended for it to be therapy. I simply made a goal to write and publish something new, every day for an entire year. And, I found that when my primary list of musings was used up, and all my initial hilarious and insightful rants were scratched off the list, I naturally began delving deeper and deeper into who I was and what had made me the person that I am.

Overcoming the demons and ghosts that made me be strangely okay with killing myself slowly? That shit took me *years*, and the majority of it didn't happen until I began writing. I wrote nearly a million words on my blog by the time I finally felt like I had tackled the last of the big ones. I had to dive into my relationships with my parents and my siblings. I had to confront the bullying from my past. I had to take an honest look at how I viewed romantic love. I had to challenge the sexual abuse I experienced as a child. I had to tackle the sexual attraction I sometimes felt toward men. My feelings about the religion in which I was brought up, and the dogmatic subculture that surrounded me had to be dealt with as well.

That can't all be done in one good sit-down, or even ten. It takes time. And the more broken you are, the more time it takes.

The good news is, I didn't have to completely fix myself to start seeing the benefits of it. The healthier I made myself mentally, the easier physical health became for me in general. The more ghosts I exorcized, the more I fell in love with my body and my physical abilities and potential. By the time I zapped the last of the big ones, I was to a point in my life where I *longed* for daily exercise and I *loved* eating healthy. There was no longer any need for rationalization or explanation. There was no need to think about diets or goals or plans. Health just became a natural part of me.

And you know what? I can honestly say that my family *does* have fat genes. I'm still convinced of it. But I don't think we have 350 lb. fat genes. We just have *chubby* fat genes, and I know now that I can be a little pudgy and still be in incredible health. I will never be a Calvin Klein underwear model. I have learned this. I will also never be Billy Currington or Bradley Cooper. But I don't have to look like those guys to be loved or thought beautiful by the masses nor do I have to look like them to be appreciated and respected by my much smaller groups of friends and loved ones.

"OL." I'm fairly certain it meant "over the limit." And I was over the limit. For a lot of things.

Precious Cargo

Pamela, the grumpy, old, fat, perma-scowling nurse was staring me down as I entered the room where my son had just been born without me. She had a bit of an evil sneer forcing the corners of her lips to tighten. Her look was just enough to tell me she had won and there was nothing I could do about it now.

Exactly nine minutes earlier, I had been in that room and Noah was still safely crammed up inside his womb. My wife, the birth mother (whom I shall call Jess), and Pamela had all been arguing about whether or not I should be allowed to watch the birth of my own child.

Pamela felt strongly that it was *completely* inappropriate. The birth mother was only 17 years old, after all, and she wouldn't stand by and let such innocence be destroyed.

Jess was turning 18 the next day. She didn't care if I was in the room, in fact, she invited me to watch the birth and never acted like it was weird or that she was uncomfortable with it.

My wife really wanted me in there as well.

It had gotten a little tense as I stood against the far wall of the delivery room, waiting for a winner to emerge. I couldn't really say anything. It wasn't my vagina I'd be watching be torn to shreds, after all.

At that point, Jess was dilated to 3 cm. There was plenty of time for them to discuss it, and eventually the perma-scowling nurse asked if I'd leave so that the women could discuss it without me hovering. I was a little annoyed. *Meh.* Who am I kidding. I wanted to give her a good swift steel-toed kick to her dangerously large caboose. I mean, did she really think I'd get my jollies off of that?

I had seen that crap in Health class. It traumatized me for years. There is *nothing* sexy I can think of in watching a woman's downstairs stretch, rip, and bleed as it forces a tiny gunky purple person through it. And no, the fact that she was still illegal by one day didn't make it more exciting to my apparently perverted mind.

What *was* exciting was that the tiny gunky purple person was going to be my son. My *son!* Our gift from his birth mom. I was going to be a daddy. And if a man has the chance, every dad should get to witness the moment his child enters the world, takes his first breath, and screams his first scream.

Damn that Pamela. I'm not still bitter or anything, but fuck her.

I bit my tongue and left the room. A Snickers bar sounded good right then.

In the five minutes I was gone, apparently Jess went from 3 cm to 10 cm and she delivered the baby. I was not in the room. And I am not exaggerating on the amount of time.

I watched as nurses and doctors rushed past me as I started downing my candy bar. I saw the door slam behind them. I went and listened at the door as pandemonium ensued and eventually my new baby boy began crying on the other side. I would learn later that Jess only had to push twice or so, and Noah came sloshing out with very little effort. I don't know if he was sick of listening to the women bicker or if he had inherited my claustrophobia, but he had had enough, and he wanted out.

I stood at the door more annoyed than a Girl Scout whose wagon full of cookies just got pushed over by a big mean perma-scowling bully. I had *missed* the birth of my son because some old lady who was not tied to our situation *at all* had thrown a little tizzy fit.

I paced outside, thinking of everything I wanted to say to this woman, but which I knew I probably wouldn't. I worried about my son. The crying hadn't lasted long at all. I worried about his birth mom. I hadn't heard her scream during the birth or cry since. I worried about the nurses, already wondering if they had sanitized properly. I worried about...

Suddenly the door cracked open and my wife poked her head out. "He's here. And he's perfect. You can come in now."

If journaling and blogging were my greatest route toward healing from the pain in my past, in the following moments when I *became* a father, my route toward real happiness and a successful future unfolded itself to me.

The moment she spoke, I forgot all of my frustrations and annoyances. I forgot about the bitter fat woman who had ruined the most important moment of my life. I just got excited. And giddy. And I took a deep breath and slipped quietly inside to see what precious cargo lied within. I first caught Pamela's victorious sneer as I entered. Then I forgot she existed at all.

My son was there, naked and wrinkly and pink, laying on a blanket inside a plastic bin. I'm sure there is another name for it that sounds more romantic, but that's what it was. A plastic bin. And still, it was magical. I just stared at him forever, anxious to hold him for the first time.

When they finally laid his little swaddled body into my eager arms, an immediate bond formed with that boy. A mantle of responsibility and love blanketed me and I vowed in my head that I would be the best dad the world has ever seen. I vowed that this boy would never know a dad that didn't love him. He would never not feel protected. He would always be mine. And I would always be his.

But that wasn't the only poignant thing I felt and experienced in that moment.

Suddenly all the stupid stuff, the illegal stuff, the immature stuff, the immoral stuff, *everything* I had ever done up to that point in my life didn't matter. It wasn't me. None of it. Not anymore.

I innately knew that *that* moment was a true new beginning for this baby *and* for his dad. The past didn't matter. It didn't exist. Not as I looked at this tiny little "thing" in my hands. And I was changed in an instant.

I learned that while they are rare, there will be moments in life when I will experience something so powerful that I can literally become a new person. Instantly.

I call them my new life opportunities. I believe everyone experiences them.

These opportunities give us the chance to straightaway become better people. We can leave the tainted parts of our pasts behind us and move forward with one resolve and one purpose.

Whether we choose to *take* those new life opportunities or not is up to each of us. Whether we choose to *see* those opportunities at all depends on how in tune we are with the validity of our past and our present. Whether we choose to *embrace* those opportunities and believe in the wonders that they are, depends on our ability to leave behind our weird need to be victims as well as our capacity to walk away from our addiction to fears.

I can only suppose that new life opportunities such as the one I had that day come pounding on all sorts of people's doors, and they tragically never even know they were there. It's as if they are too busy watching their daily soaps to bother answering the door when the old dude with the giant check shows up on their porch. And they miss out on them altogether.

I am so thankful I was able to *see* my new life opportunity for what it was, and that I wasn't so set in my ways, so eager to embrace my imperfections, and so attached to the old me that I couldn't accept the gift I was being given.

I am so thankful that I got up from my stupid-life TV show and answered the door when the guy with the check came knocking. What was delivered to me was both rare and incredible, and I will never lack appreciation for that single unrepeatable moment of my life.

Another Pointless List of
My Random Thoughts

And now, the second half of that pointless list of my random thoughts.

- Avid women hikers don't wear bras. I've never been sure why.
- Men in hot yoga classes don't care when their balls hang out of their shorts. I've also never been sure why.
- Most of us are much more content debating what we know reality television stars should be doing to fix their problems than we are fixing the equally daunting problems in our own lives and relationships.
- Beards make some guys ultra-sexy. Some guys they just help not to look like giant overgrown babies. When properly trimmed, beards are appreciated by most everyone and have their popularity ups and downs from one generation to the next.
- Mustaches have been creepy in every generation.
- Some men are so lazy and so entitled that they refuse to wait for an open urinal in public restrooms and then they pee all over the unlifted seat in the sit-down stall. These men should be court-ordered into a "learn to be less douchey and entitled" course.

- When some bloggers feel inadequate or inferior, they become monster jerks to other bloggers on the Internet. They *try* to make their motives appear pure and humble. They're really just insecure ass hats. Anyone can start a blog. Even insecure ass hats.

- Getting super drunk is fun. If, that is, fun includes activities such as: dancing without inhibition; drinking shots out of someone else's scrotum; singing the best karaoke rendition of *Pianoman* you or anyone else in that bar has ever heard; laughing uncontrollably; crying uncontrollably; taking your pants off and running around like a hooligan; kissing complete strangers; having the best sex ever; having the worst sex ever; having sex you don't remember having; getting pregnant and not knowing how or when it happened; regretful exes getting clingier; angry exes getting angrier; puking; forgetting things; and more. Drink responsibly, people. You don't actually *want* to be sipping booze out of that random guy's scrotum. I promise you.

- People on the Internet who get so heated and intense about politics and religion annoy *everyone*. They should really go find a different Internet.

- At the gym there are so many mostly chiseled, sexy, perfectly figured men and women. They are everywhere you turn and they make you feel ugly and fat no matter how fit you are. Nobody actually knows where these people go after they leave the gym, or if they even exist in real life at all because they're rarely spotted in public.

- The majority of ugly and horrible comments on YouTube videos (and there are a *lot* of them) seem to be made mostly by men in Asia. Again, I've never been sure why. I get the idea they get their jollies ruffling our easily rufflable Western feathers.

- To the vast majority of the human population, Twitter doesn't make any sense no matter how much they try to learn it and appreciate it. Present company included.

- Sex is fun. I didn't used to think it was, nor did I understand why people liked it so much. That was back when I was too lazy to take my socks off while doing the deed. I feel bad for any woman who bedded me back then.

- People who chain smoke in casinos all day every day don't have anything positive to say when well-fed giant white men attempt to strike up friendly conversations. I am also somewhat convinced these people are made of rotting cardboard.

- There are people who buy book after book after book. They keep them on their bookshelves, their titles displayed side by side like trophies. They've also never gotten around to reading more than two or three of them. I am one such person.

- Women appreciate it when you keep a box of mints on the bed stand. Believe me, they often want to jump your bones when they wake up, but they don't want to be passing that nasty morning jank breath back and forth.

- Bullies still exist, even in the grown-up world. They need just as much love as kid bullies do.

- No matter how dumb a person is, I promise you he or she is smarter than me at something.

- When someone constantly tells you what a nice person they are, they're probably not a very nice person.

- When someone constantly tells you what an honest person they are, they're probably not a very honest person.

- When someone constantly tells you what a generous person they are, you guessed it. They're probably not a very generous person.

- When anyone constantly tells you what an *any kind* of person they are, they're probably trying to convince themselves that they're something they know they're not, but that they wish they were. Just nod your head and say, "I'll be the judge of that." It will drive them crazy.

- Cops don't like when they have to work on major holidays. Be extra careful not to get caught in the crosshairs of their bad attitudes on the following days: Easter. Christmas. Thanksgiving. And, for some reason, September 3rd.

- We have gadgets in our lives that even ten years ago we couldn't have envisioned. Yet, every time something new is released, our currently prized gadgets become worthless and ancient pieces of junk to us. We all need to go back to 1992 for a few weeks and realize the miracles that are now running our everyday lives for us.

- If you are single and you want to accidentally bump into other single people, the baking aisle at the grocery store is *not* the place to do it. Try the frozen foods or canned soup sections instead.

- I have decided that only two kinds of guys still wear spray-on deodorant. Guys with mustaches and guys with mullets.

Changing

I've spent too much of this book talking about sordid things already, and *way* too much of this book talking about moments that involved number twos.

That being said, I bring you one more glorious chapter surrounding bodily functions. Get through this with me, and I promise I'll *try* not to be overly gross throughout the rest of these stories.

Besides, *this* chapter is about baby yuck, which is cute. I guess.

But before I get into that, let me tell you that once as a grown man, I soiled my pants at a Golden Corral.

Meh. Let's all be honest with each other for a moment. When you're a grown ass man, and you defecate in your bloomers, the *only* term that will do for it is "shit your pants." You didn't have an accident. You didn't have a slip-up. You didn't poop yourself. You straight-up *shit* your pants, and it's something you need to man-up to with the proper terminology, no matter if you've got a foul mouth or not.

So, let me rephrase. Once, as a grown man, I shit myself at a Golden Corral. I'm not going to get into details (you're welcome). Just know that it was the absolute, 100% most *horrible* and humiliating experience of my life. It was one of those "aaaaaalllmost make it" situations which ended in a giant mess and yours truly covered in his own, well, you get the idea.

I don't tell you this for any reason than that it's integral to some of the lessons I learned later on as a brand new dad.

And most of those lessons came while changing my kid's diapers.

I have nine siblings, six of which are sisters. I am second oldest of the brood, so as a young teenager I had to change a *lot* of diapers. My youngest three sisters were all in diapers at the same time, and that meant everyone had to pitch in if anyone wanted to keep their sanity for long.

Back then, I found changing diapers to be a horrible and suffocating task. I loathed it and counted down the days until my sisters could control their own faculties.

Then I had a baby boy of my own and I realized something. Changing baby girl diapers is *nothing* in comparison to changing those of baby boys.

As we prepared to bring Noah home from the hospital, I stood in the new nursery we had decorated for him and surveyed the room. Over in the corner was a Diaper Genie. More than a hundred newborn diapers were neatly stacked in rows on the shelf next to it. I'd be changing a lot of diapers, but it wouldn't be too bad. I wouldn't loathe it the way I had when I was a teenager. Not when it was my own kid.

But nothing could have prepared me for what was coming.

I certainly never experienced changing diapers full of the thick black tar that filled his nappies the first few days. The pungent stench from it still troubles me. It smelled the way I'd imagine it would if I stuck my head neck-deep into the mostly eaten remains of a zebra that the lions had finished off three days prior. I've been assured this is completely normal for newborns.

I also never had to figure out what the hell to do with a baby erection while changing any of my sisters.

And if you're looking for answers, I don't have them. I still have no idea what to do when you go to change your baby boy and he's got a little hard-on. There's nothing right about that. Babies shouldn't get those. I don't care how natural and normal it is. I'm telling you, they shouldn't get those.

My wife always used to tell me, "it's just like morning wood, get over it."

"You get over it!" I'd yell as I squinted one eye and examined the poop that was coating the dang thing. "It ain't right, I tell you. It ain't right!"

I'd half-heartedly swish a baby wipe around it, and my heart would always sink when it did nothing to clean it. I'd then whip his erection with the baby wipe over and over, *willing* the poop to come off. That never worked either. Usually I'd stand and wait for the longest time, willing the boner to go away. That also never worked. I have decided that baby erections last just short of *forever*.

Eventually, I'd get a fresh baby wipe, bite my bottom lip, close my eyes, and give it a good scrub until it was clean.

I never felt like a dirtier man. It ain't right, I tell you. It ain't right. In my perfect universe, stiffies won't even be possible until a man is 30 or so.

But stiffies weren't the only thing for which I was ill-prepared. I had heard many stories of little boys peeing while their diapers were being changed, but until you experience it first hand, you'll never understand what I now do.

Let's start with the speed at which they can pee. Count to one. See how fast you did that? Well, that wasn't as fast as a baby boy can pee when you open up his diaper, so let's do another exercise. Snap your fingers. Nope. Still not fast enough. Let's try blinking your eyes. Yeah… *still* not fast enough. I know because once Noah got me in the eye before I could even close them to protect myself.

And while the speed is frightening, the incredible aim is straight-up terrifying. I'm telling you, my son had complete control over his tallywacker, and it didn't matter which way I jumped to dodge his urine, he would aim that thing straight at me. I could jump left or right. He'd nail me. Forward or back. He'd get me. I could be standing four feet away dropping his cargo into the diaper bin, and somehow he'd hit me there, too. That kid never missed.

And that was okay, I suppose. It gave me funny stories to tell around the dinner table, and over time I learned how to somehow change his diapers without ever leaving his loaded cannon exposed and free to fire.

But Noah wasn't content with that. I could see in his expression that he found it funny to hose down his old man. His eyes would get giant and bright and he'd develop the slightest little grin. I could also sense his frustration when I began thwarting his every attack. It was almost as if he'd scowl at me slightly when I changed him, upset that I was taking away his fun.

Then one day, my baby exploded.

I had just successfully changed his diaper. No erection. No pee in the eye. No incident whatsoever.

I scooped him off of the table and held him against me. That's when he grunted the tiniest, cutest little grunt.

All future dads, listen up and let me save you some serious grossness in your future. If your baby grunts, set him down and run.

Babies don't grunt. Ever. Unless, that is, they are about to push out the biggest diarrhea explosion of their young little lives.

And that's what Noah did. After he grunted, I held him out in front of me and began laughing at the face he started making. He squinted one eye, clamped his mouth shut, looked me dead in the eyes, and grunted once more. Only this wasn't a cute grunt. This was a *man* grunt.

And then he exploded.

With one powerful pop, baby diarrhea went airborne in every direction. It shot from both leg holes of his diaper, and it shot straight up his back. It shot hard, it shot hot, and it shot fast. And, I just happened to be standing in the line of fire for *all* of it.

It took me a minute to realize what had happened. There was poop on my neck. There was poop all over my arms and shirt. There was poop on my sweatpants.

I tried not to vomit as I held the nasty little creature who had just done something so impossibly horrid out in front of me. He was even more covered than I was, but his face was completely melted and relaxed. He was at peace and he was happy.

I wanted to start screaming in disgust, but I could only laugh. "Come quick!" I yelled to my wife who was absorbed in her daytime TV talk shows two rooms away. "Come quick and bring the camera with you! Hurry!" She came running and we both laughed harder than we had in a long time.

I learned a lesson that day. And it was a big one.

Shit happens. And sometimes really bad shit happens.

When it does, sometimes *all* we can do is clean it up as best we can, and have a good laugh about it.

Yes, sometimes shit is stressful and hard and maybe even life altering. Sometimes before we can have our good laugh, we need to have a good cry about it first. I assure you I cried the night I shit my pants at the Golden Corral. The stress and the anxiety of it all had gotten to me that badly.

But, that moment in time passed. The horrible present became my really funny past. And it doesn't usually matter what happens in our lives; when enough time has passed, we can always still laugh about how ridiculous and humiliating and crazy those moments were.

Twice I was covered in explosive grossness. And I can promise you this. Sometimes the only real difference between a hilarious situation and a traumatic one is attitude.

My First (and Last) Attempt to
Spank My Kid

Back in the 80s, there was a popular game people played at the beach called Smashball. I don't know how the game worked. I only know that when you purchased a Smashball set, it came with two giant wooden paddles and a small blue rubber ball.

In large blue letters across each paddle was the word *Smashball*. I remember those paddles well. Yellow plastic handles, pine finish, not really smooth, yet not really rough, and just the right amount of surface area to cover a kid's entire backside.

As far as I know, Mom and Dad never actually played Smashball with those paddles. They kept one paddle on the dark hardwood dresser in their bedroom, and another on the kitchen counter, wedged between the toaster and the fridge. Whenever we did something wrong, they sent us off to fetch whichever paddle was closer. Whenever we did something *really* wrong, they sent us to fetch the further paddle so that we had more time to anxiously anticipate the walloping reprimand to come. Okay, that last part was made-up. But if I was into paddling my kids, that's how I'd do it.

To say I was spanked a lot as a child would be like saying RuPaul is gay. It's true, but again... It's not as magnificently true as it could be. There needs to be a few more imaginative adjectives jammed in to make it a more precise statement.

Due to my extremely strong will and my vast expertise in the ways of naughtiness and mischief growing up, I got a *lot* of spankings, and for some reason I got two or three times the spankings any of my nine siblings did. I don't think the last half of the kids found themselves on the receiving end of a single half-solid swat, and definitely never with the Smashball paddle. This wasn't necessarily because my parents didn't want to spank them, but because by the late eighties, spanking was becoming frowned upon by society as a whole, and Mom and Dad were left with nubs for hands from all of the corporal punishment that I was constantly being dished.

And it wasn't just Smashball paddles that they used. As early as my childhood memories take me, I was sent off to grab shoes, wooden spoons, and magazines. If I was lucky, I'd bend over and get a couple whoopin's on my covered rear end. If I had been naughty enough, I was made to yank my pants down, bend over, grab my ankles, and take a set of them on the bare cheeks.

If I fought with Eric or Tomi Ann, I got a whoopin'. If I went around chanting "do you hear the wind?" every time my kid sister Amy spoke, I'd get a whoopin'. If I didn't do my chores, I'd get a whoopin'. If I talked back to Mom or Dad, you guessed it. I got a whoopin'.

It's not lost on me that those paragraphs make my parents seem like absolute tyrants who loved beating the shit out of their kids. I've never thought this was true at all. It was a different time back then. Just about every parent whooped their kids and nobody really thought twice about. I'm just thankful I missed the old "go cut a switch off the willow tree" era. I'd take a Smashball paddle over a raw branch-shaped welt any day of the week.

Of course, nowadays, if you spank your child, you *must* be a bad parent. This is evident by all the perfect parents out there on the Internet telling us so.

But I don't think that's true either. In truth, it saddens me sometimes that we live in a day in which we are raising entitled, wussy, snobby kids who don't know how to work, who don't know manners, and who don't know what it means to respect one's elders.

Everywhere I go, I see children screaming at their parents, those parents giving into their children's tantrums and demands, and parents in general having no idea *what* to do to get their kids under control. Parents are really beginning to fear the word "no," and that scares the living hell out of me. I can't help but think we're headed into a future in which those who could be truly great do nothing at all because they don't know how to do anything but stamp their feet for what they want.

Don't get me wrong. The no spanking movement isn't a bad one. I do believe that there are so many better ways to handle almost all problems with your kids. We live in a time when there are countless books, parenting courses, seminars, websites, blogs, and podcasts, all which point to better ways. But that doesn't mean that nobody should *ever* spank their kids. In the words of our family counselor way back once upon a time when I was married, "sometimes it's the only thing that works, so long as you're in control when you do."

To me, crossing the line would be using spanking too often, and while one's out of control, as a tool to control children with fear. Doing so installs lifelong resentment in kids, self-esteem issues, and inability to communicate properly. But don't take my word for it, go Google the phrase, "negative effects of spanking." Just beware of those few crazy and perfect Internet parents who will make you feel as worthless as possible if you do spank your kids from time to time.

As for me, I grew up in crazy fear of Mom, Dad, and that Smashball paddle. Most of the time they didn't even have to use it. A simple "do you wanna have to go get the paddle?" would stop just about any bickering. But when I did get it, oh how I got it. And oh how I hated them in those moments. I would sometimes sit on my bed for hours with tear stained cheeks, feeling nothing but injustice and disdain for them. I made myself the promise hundreds of times that *I* would never spank *my* kids.

I always tease Mom and Dad that it's not fair that they stopped spanking when their younger kids came around. Secretly, I'm genuinely happy that they did. Nobody should be spanked as much as I was, not even kids who were as stubborn and resistant and as hard to get along with as I was.

Now I'm the parent, and I have my own kid to discipline.

And Noah, he's a different cat when it comes to the need for punishment. Sure, he has his naughty moments, but Daddy believes in the warning system for most things, and Noah almost never needs more than one warning to stop a poor behavior. It's not uncommon for him to go an entire month or two without a timeout. He helps when I ask him to help. He goes to bed when I say it's bedtime. He eats when I say it's time to eat. He keeps his bedroom clean.

But, he's far from perfect (thank God). Even the easiest of kids can have their out of control crazy "moments." And Noah had a doozy several years ago when we were staying at a condo on vacation in Southern California with the rest of my family.

We had spent the day at the beach, and as a group we had half-dragged ourselves crispy and worn-out back to the condo. Noah was completely caked in all sorts of sand and sea crap, and I told him to follow me for a quick bath.

He had been promised pizza, and there was no convincing him that the bath would be over and done with way before the pizza got there. His stubbornness and crying got worse and then became something beyond the definition of a tantrum. It turned into something so horrible that there isn't a word in the English language for it. Just know that it was bad. And he was *completely* out of control.

I was quickly running out of patience. As sand was chaffing my own butt cheeks, and my flesh oozed heat from overexposure, I began losing my tolerance for his outburst.

I picked his flailing body up and set him in the tub. Then, I took a breath and warned him. "Noah, if you don't settle down before I count to three, you're going to get an uh-oh." Uh-Ohs are what we call timeouts in this house.

He continued his fit. I attempted the timeout which only caused the out-of-control toddler to slip deeper into his rabies-like insanity. "Noah, if you don't calm down, you're going to get a spanking." He had never had one before, but he knew very well what they were because he had a step-sister who got them sometimes.

He kept going, and so I grabbed his arm and pulled him erect. He flopped and thrashed out of control to try and avoid the inevitable slap on his bare wet bottom, but I was determined to follow through. I managed to give him a little smack dead center of his left cheek (so soft, in fact, it probably wouldn't have killed a mosquito).

Instantly, the commotion died, and the whole bathroom went silent. My grip loosened and he quickly and quietly slumped out of my reach, defeated.

Noah sat in the ever-coldening bathwater, and soon forced a gaze at me. His eyes got big. Bigger than I'd ever seen them. Enormous crocodile tears surfaced at the corners. His tiny voice cracked, and he barely got out the words. "Daddy, why did you hit me?"

The look of betrayal in his eyes was more than I could feel okay with. I instantly thought back to all the promises I had made myself when I was a child. I thought back to my bed and the hours spent laying in it, resenting my parents. And I knew I had *attempted* to spank him more from a place of frustrated anger and less from a place of control.

I panicked and scooped him out of the tub and hugged him close to me, rubbing the site of the assault. "I'm sorry buddy, I slipped, I didn't mean to. It was an accident. Daddy would *never* hit you."

It was an accident?" he asked.

"Yeah," I replied.

He slinked back into the bathtub and finished without incident. I was left with my own thoughts as I washed the California grime from his body.

I had wimped out. And not just a little. I had taken the coward's approach to parenting. In that moment, I had become two things. I had become the kind of parent I can't stand, and I had become what I had always promised I wouldn't. I had become the part of my parents that I always had resented. I had seen it in his eyes when I did. I had betrayed him the same way my parents used to betray me with that giant wooden paddle.

That bothered me. But I can honestly say it didn't bother me as much as the fact that I didn't own up to it.

I definitely learned something that night.

I learned that despite our best efforts, sometimes we *all* become that which we fear most from our past, even if in small degrees.

Instead of pretending for my own ego that it wasn't what it was, I should have acknowledged it, apologized for it, and simply done *better* the next time. Covering it up didn't do anyone any favors. It didn't leave room for me to improve.

Had I told the truth, Noah would have forgiven me, and he also would have learned a couple valuable lessons himself. He would have learned that Dad means business, and he also would have learned that Dad recognizes when he himself isn't perfect and that he's willing to admit that.

It was my first and last attempt at spanking my kid, and as almost silly as it was, the lesson has carried with me heavily ever since.

The Golden Ticket

If you were to ask me what the three happiest days of my life have been so far, I wouldn't even have to think about it. Before you even finished asking, I would man-grunt just as my answer came bursting out of me in all directions, and you'd find yourself covered in a thick goopy layer of what I would say are the moments at the top of my list.

Top spot goes to the day my kid was born. And I'm not saying that in an "I'm a dad and I know it's the *correct* thing to say" sort of way. There is no question about it. The day Noah was born is one for the history books. This world became a brighter place that day. Light and laughter somehow entered even the darkest corners. The devil himself nearly gave up and went home for good. Oh, I may change my mind about some of that when he rounds the bend to teenager. We'll see. But right now, the day he entered my life definitely gets the number one spot. And yes, I will happily accept the much-coveted Biggest Cheese Award now.

Second place goes to the day I officially left the Mormon church. Now, I'm sure there will be lots of Mormons reading this, including many of my best friends and family, who will be so sad to hear that. But don't take it personally. The reason it was one of the best days was because for the first time in my life, I declared to the entire world that I believe something different, and I am going to follow my *own* beliefs now, come what may. I knew it would lead to a shit storm of resentment and pressure. I knew it would alienate me from a lot of people that I love. I knew that it would make me an outsider from the majority of the society I live in, which is *why* it took so long for me to do, and equally is why it was such a happy thing for me to finally declare. I am convinced that nothing brings a person happiness faster than a life of true authenticity, whatever the hell that looks like.

The third and final happiest day of my life may surprise you. It definitely surprised me. And it goes to the day that I found out my wife had been having an affair.

I know, I know. Affairs are supposed to end us emotionally and mentally. They are supposed to rip open our hearts and leave us bloodied and bruised and wanting to disappear from the face of the earth. It's even understandable that they leave so many of us temporarily senseless or even slightly murderous. But not her affair. Not to me.

I never once was angry with her, nor did I feel betrayed. In so many ways I was just thankful. Our marriage had taken us to the point where one of us had to do something drastic to get out because neither one of us wanted to admit that it just wasn't ever going to work.

We also couldn't call it quits because divorce is *very* frowned upon for any reason outside of infidelity or abuse when you're a Mormon. And I don't say that lightly. People literally *frown* at you if they find out you're getting a divorce. As if heavy weights were attached to the corners of their mouths, their lips droop impossibly downward. Their eyes half-squint. Their nostrils flare ever so slightly. Their eyebrows scrunch. And they look at you as if to say, "I bet you deal drugs and don't pay taxes and kill babies, too." I call them righteous frowns, and they have always given me the serious willies.

But throw an extramarital affair from your soon to be ex on there, and you can expect casseroles delivered to your doorstep for the next month!

As people, we *love* affairs.

We don't love the thought of them. We don't love when they're being had by people who are supposed to love the people we love. We definitely don't love them when they hurt and break-apart families. But we *do* love them.

We love to talk about affairs and mix them into our gossip. We love to jump in and dissect the whos, whats, whens, wheres, whys, and hows. We love to point fingers and cast blame. We love to cry out, "I knew that bastard was a cheater from the day I laid eyes on him!" We love the opportunities they give us to shake our heads and feel superior to others.

Affairs are the golden ticket in divorce. They're the one thing we can take and wildly shake in front of the whole world as we declare, "see! It's not my fault this marriage ended!" When your spouse cheats, it is so easy to make the entire world love you and hate her. The world *cheers* for you in your divorce. They understand it, and they don't fight against it. They justify your divorce for you so that you don't have to do it.

It's why so many people hold onto the affairs for so long. As a single dad who has been in the dating scene for many years now, I can tell you that the vast majority of divorcees I have dated immediately went for the cheating jugular of their exes during our dinner conversations. "Yes, I'm divorced. I discovered he had been cheating on me with three different women, two men, and a freaky thing he met at the circus, gender and species unknown." I have no idea if their exes even actually had affairs, but hey. When you're meeting someone new and you have to admit that you once fell in love and committed your entire life to someone *else*, you often feel like you need that golden ticket to make yourself datable and loveable once again.

Me, I always like to shock the women I dated. "Oh, my wife had an affair, too." The girl would always look at me as if to say, *oh phew. This guy is datable. It wasn't his fault.* Then I continue. "Oh yeah, it was one of the best days of my life! We couldn't stand each other. We treated each other like crap. We didn't do much of anything to help or save our marriage. We stopped caring about each other pretty much at all. We became selfish and self-absorbed." At this point I take a breath in, indicating that I was going to keep talking whether she liked it or not. She'd look at me as if to say *is this guy serious right now?* And I'd continue.

"We were young and stupid and didn't know how to be good people to each other. We didn't know what love even was when we got married. We were idiots." Her eyes would untighten a little. *Maybe this guy isn't so bad. I mean, he seems to get it.* And I'd carry on. "I don't blame her for the affair. I never have. She did us both a favor to get us out of a desperate situation." *Boom.* She usually at this point decides that she kind of likes me and is ready to disrobe right then and there.

Because, you see, everyone with a portion of a brain knows that affairs are rarely black and white. Even those whose spouses cheated know deep down that it probably wasn't as cut and dry as they often let on. And, it's a bit of a heavy burden to constantly flash that golden ticket to everyone you meet while *never* taking even a dollop of responsibility for oneself.

Yes, it is true. Some people really are just cheating assholes who don't give a shit about the person they're with. I get that it happens.

But from what I have witnessed, many more affairs are the byproduct of relationships gone sour. They're done out of a need for love, the need to be touched and admired, the need to be desired, and the very real need for sex. Many affairs are exactly what my wife's affair most likely was. An act of desperation which she knew would have a good chance in ending the marriage. It was a saving grace for both of us.

Of course it's usually going to be better to work on the relationship and to fix the relationship. But sometimes it's impossible. For us, I have no doubt that at that juncture of our lives, it was impossible.

We both were too stubborn to go see a counselor. We both were too caught up on the notion that we gave up our youth and our entire lives to the other, not knowing fully well what we were getting into. We both wanted the perfect marriage without the work. We both were immature little brats who seemed to work relentlessly to self-sabotage our marriage over the years so that we could one day get out of it.

I'm just old enough and barely wise enough now to see that and to admit that.

We were young. We were dumb. And it wasn't going to fix itself. We both needed to step away from the mess we originally stepped into in order to realize just what it was we were, and what it was we were doing to each other.

I never lied to the women I've dated as a single man since. I've told the blatant truth about my divorces (yes, I've had two of them). And surprise of surprises, they nearly always appreciated me all the more for that.

The happiness I felt the day I found out my wife was having the affair was no different than the happiness I felt when I left the church I was born into. It was the feeling of freedom from a life that wasn't actually my own. We had both changed so much in opposite directions that we didn't want our entire lives to be tied to each other anymore. We weren't compatible. We would not ever find happiness or contentment, nor the ability to personally grow and mature so long as we were together. We had discovered enough of ourselves to know that if we went back in time, knowing what we know now, we never would have gotten together in the first place.

The lessons I learned were many. It took another fleeting rebound marriage and a lot of the exact same mistakes to really learn those lessons, too.

Rarely is the end of any marriage or relationship black and white. Mine certainly wasn't. As a population, I believe we need to stop waving those giant affair flags as we declare that we had no part in the demise of our relationships and our marriages. To do so makes us victims, and when we remain victims, we *cannot* grow.

I think it's okay be sad and angry when our partners have extramarital affairs. We probably *should* be sad and angry. But when we're done with that, we need to stand up, dust ourselves off, and look at what part, as small as it might be, that we might have played in it all. We need to move past it, forgive, and stop using it as our impermeable shields against the judgments of outsiders. We need to do it for our own sakes.

That is *difficult* I know. After all, affairs *are* that golden ticket to appear perfect and not at all like failures in our relationships. But we should ask ourselves one question. Do we want our next relationships to be with a complete victim who takes no responsibility for his or her part in things? Or do we want it to be with someone who owns their own shit and continually improves on it?

I am not making excuses for those who have affairs. And I am definitely not saying that if we want to give our partners the happiest days of their lives, we should go hop in bed with someone else. No, no, no. When we commit ourselves to someone, and we promise not to boink other people, it's a pretty damn good idea to keep that promise.

Personally, I think that if we find ourselves at the point of desperation where we feel like we need an affair in our lives, we should do something else desperate instead. We should tell our partners, whom we were once so in love with, *what* we're being tempted with and how desperate and broken we are feeling.

I promise you, *that* conversation will either make or break the relationship, and isn't that what we really want at that point? For it to be fixed or broken, once and for all?

The lessons from my past scream to me. Don't become someone else's golden ticket. Don't use cheating assholes as my own golden ticket. Our lives are our own. We each make or break every part of them. Whether we choose to let the actions of others keep us broken or to let them ultimately strengthen us is completely up to each of us.

As for me, I've learned what and who I want in the future. I want a person who is now a champion of her past. Not a victim who never could let go of it to put herself back together again.

Famous and Popular {at Last}

Somewhere between the affair and becoming *oh* so fabulous and famous (which I'll get to), I got both married and divorced to another woman. This is what I learned from that extremely brief stint in my life.

Don't get married on the rebound. Weekly or semi-weekly therapy gets *really* expensive, and if it ain't working after a year, it probably ain't gonna work at all. Certain mother-in-laws have the ability to make life gloriously awful. Redheads can be extremely beautiful *and* extremely feisty. Have quieter sex when your brother and his family are staying as guests in your home. And, it hurts really, really bad to get close to a child and have her suddenly disappear from your life.

But this chapter is not actually about that part of my life. It's about me becoming famous. And popular. And renowned. And celebrated. I simply felt I had to stick *something* in here *somewhere* about my marriage number two. After all, it did happen. I guess. And it was the worthlessness I felt as a twice-divorced newly single dad that pushed me to start my blog which very quickly brought me my fame.

Single Dad Laughing. That is my blog. I know I don't even have to tell you the name of it. That would be like Tom Hanks telling you he was in Sleepless in Seattle or Kim Kardashian telling you she has a nice ass. You already know. *Everyone* already knows.

Am I coming off as a complete jerk yet? Good.

I started my blog days after my wife tore-off down the street in our minivan, leaving me standing on the driveway, holding my confused son, feeling like the most valueless and miserable wreck on earth.

Remember those evil righteous frowns I told you about? The ones that people around here hand-out like Halloween candy when someone gets divorced? Well, this was divorce number *two* for me. The frowns get heavier and fatter on round two, only they start being accompanied by what I call righteous *eyes*. Above that frown, the eyes would somehow bulge while squinting, and they would say one of two things. Either, "there's obviously something seriously wrong with you," or "Dear God, please don't touch me. I don't want your failure to rub off on me and ruin *my* life and marriage, too." This is usually supplemented with a barely detectible nervous head twitch and heavy breathing.

And so, in the thick of my insecurities about being divorced twice at the age of 30, I started my blog. Within a few months, I was writing entries that were going mega-viral. People were reading by the tens of thousands and then by the hundreds of thousands. I was being blogged about and talked about and discussed and heralded all over the internet. My Facebook fan page went from a few hundred to more than 30,000 all within the course of a month or two.

And suddenly, I was *famous*.

Women would now certainly beg to be with me. Friends would line up around blocks. I would be mobbed everywhere I went. It was finally my turn to be and have everything I deserved after so many trials and so much hard work.

Except… I wasn't famous at all, and I seemed to be the *only* one who didn't know that.

This is what I remember from my "thought I was famous" stage of life.

- I would walk around grocery stores and shopping malls looking *everyone* dead in the eye as they walked past, creepily and mentally encouraging them to recognize me and make a fuss over my existence.

- I turned down all *sorts* of interviews by local television shows and radio programs and bloggers who were so much smaller than I was because I was too big-time to deal with such small-time nuisances.

- A producer from *The Ellen Show* called after I pompously coerced my fans into flooding Ellen and Oprah with requests to have me on. After five minutes on the phone with me, he hung up and never contacted me again because I was an arrogant nitwit.

- I quit my really high paying job because, well, I was famous and I didn't need it. After all, fame comes with a healthy side of opportunity, and I knew there would be plenty of it.

- If a woman I was dating didn't become a huge fan herself, I lost interest. She needed to think I walked on water just like everyone else obviously did.

- I drove my family crazy. I drove my friends crazy. I drove every woman I dated crazy. Their annoyance with me was obviously based in jealousy.

- I got a license plate that said SDL on it because I knew endless people would see those initials and honk and wave because they loved my blog so much.

- I expected everything to just work in my favor without much further effort or thought from me. I expected free stuff from everyone. I wanted everything done for me. Even little things became annoying like having to butter my own toast or fill up my own gas tank.

- I wore sunglasses indoors so that I wouldn't be recognized when I as in a hurry.

- Everywhere I went without sunglasses on, I had an excuse why nobody *there* was recognizing me. These people are too young. These people are too male. These people aren't parents. These people would never read blogs. These people are so old they probably don't even know what the Internet is. These girls are too stuck-up and prissy to read my kind of stuff. These guys only care about tech sites. These people just aren't (fill in pretentious and self-deluding blank, I probably thought it).

This phase lasted about a year, and if I'm being honest, I'm surprised I have any friends or family members left who will even tolerate my presence now. If any of them weren't famous at all (the way I wasn't) and started acting the way I did, I assure you I would have grabbed them by the shoulders, shook them nice and hard, slapped them up and down a few times, and told them, "get over your fucking self. No one gives a shit."

But everyone in my life was too nice to do that for me.

My fatal poison was that every so often, and not often at all, *someone, somewhere* would recognize me. I'd get occasional emails from strangers that would say things like, "I saw you at the park yesterday." Every once in a while I'd be at a party and someone I didn't know would pipe in, "hey, I know you! You're Single Dad Laughing!" and then they'd get everyone to start talking about me and my famous blog. Yes, all this happened just often enough that I was able to hold onto the illusion that I was actually famous. I led myself to believe that most people who did recognize me were too shy or respectful to say anything or to approach me. I believed that my fans were everywhere and simply too intimidated by my fame to accost me.

And, like I said. I wasn't famous, and I was the only one who didn't seem to know it.

Eventually, I accepted the fact that I had turned into a pompous, self-indulged douchebag, and I went back to regular life as the non-famous fairly enjoyable person I have always tried to be. My friendships immediately strengthened. Family dinners were more enjoyable. And I liked myself *more*. The funny thing is, once I got over myself, my blog started growing faster than it ever had before.

I've thought a lot about it since that span of my life. These are some of the many lessons I've learned or observed about fame.

- The more I learn about fame, the more I don't want it. I really don't. Nowadays I turn down interviews, reality TV shows, and many other opportunities for no other reason than that the thought of actual fame scares the living hell out of me. I've seen what being *almost* famous can do to this giant white man. I'd hate to think what would actually happen if I somehow did one day become famous.

- There are two kinds of fame. Fame for a person. And fame for a person's work. I'd much rather have my work be famous and never be recognized in public at all.

- Fame can't be measured. Not really. The most famous movie star can walk right by your grandmother and she might not recognize her. But your grandmother would recognize you. That means, to your grandmother, you're more famous than the movie star.

- When people think you're famous, they will guilt you left and right to use your fame and platform for their advantage or gain. This is especially true of people that were once, long ago, good friends.

- Having kids and being in the public eye comes with its own set of unique challenges. I have to be overly protective of my kid which isn't always fair to him.

- Becoming popular doesn't get rid of the crazy shit that runs in the background of your life. Instead, it amplifies it. Just take my word for that.

- Famous people are like cops. They're either really awesome or really big weenies.

- Popularity doesn't last without considerable ongoing effort to remain *constantly* fresh in the minds of others. This is true for famous movie stars, brands, musicians, athletes, and even the popular kids at school. I have a large blog following and I promise you, if I suddenly disappeared, very few people would notice and even fewer people would care beyond a day or two.

- People are just people, no matter how famous they are. As a blogger, I've had the opportunity to sit across from Betty White, Danny DeVito, Ed Helms, Zac Efron, and many others. Every time I do, I can't help but humorously think, what is the big deal exactly? This person is just like any other person. They've all got to take their morning tinkles just like the rest of us. They all have their insecurities, and their quirks, and their bad days, and their weaknesses. Well, everyone except Betty White. I'm pretty sure she is actually my idea of perfect.

- It doesn't matter who you are, there will be people who resent, loathe, or straight-up hate you for your popularity. This is strangely even true for Betty White. Who I secretly hope adopts me as her grandson one day.

- Nobody just gets famous. Sure, many of us will experience our 15 minutes of it without any effort, but the truly famous are there because of three things. Some sort of uniqueness. A *lot* of hard work and persistence. And more than anything else, a lot of *luck*.

- It *is* fun to be recognized by strangers so long as you're not in a giant hurry. It *is* really fun when a stranger makes a big deal about you and starts screaming and getting all crazy about your existence. This has happened to me exactly four times, and all four times were while I was shopping at Walmart. I'm not sure what to take from that.

- If you're actually famous, having fans flip out on you four times is probably more of a daily number and definitely not a lifetime achievement number.

- If you're actually famous, you probably don't shop at Walmart.

Perhaps more than anything else, I've learned that there is absolutely *nothing* wrong with being popular or famous. The danger comes when anyone truly thinks they are more important than any other human when fame or popularity happens upon them.

As for me, I've learned what I want, and it's not fame. I do have to keep constantly fresh in the lives and minds of my readers. It's how I make my living. But I don't want fame from it.

I can say with integrity that I want instead to be remembered by my friends and family as the person who showed up when it mattered most. I want to be remembered as the person who never felt himself better than they, better than he actually was, and who always looked for the true beauty in others while being very much okay with them for exactly who and what they were.

I want to be remembered by my son as the dad who was always there, the dad who truly cared for him, the dad who taught him how to work and learn, and the dad who supported him in every dream his young mind ever conjured, never stepping into a "let's be realistic about your future" mode.

I want to be remembered by the person to whom I someday devote the rest of my life as the man who always put her first, never went too long without buying her flowers, genuinely cared about the little things in her life, and who was always faithful. Oh, and as the most amazing lay she ever had. That would be nice, too.

I've spent a few years now reading the daily feedback on my blog posts and comments over social media. There were single days when millions would visit my work, thousands would leave loving and wonderful comments, and still it would mean nothing to me because I would go to bed those nights and stare across at an empty pillow next to mine, wondering how it was that if so many people loved me, I was alone at the end of the day.

To love and be loved in return. Nothing is better than that. No amount of fame. No amount of popularity. No amount of money. This is what I now know. Whether it's with your children, your partner, or your family and friends. *Nothing* is better than to love and be loved in return.

Traumatic Kiss

I'm going to more weightily examine romantic love and the quest to love and be loved in return. But first, there was this. A pointless little dating story from a different time in my life, with a *very* profound moral attached to it. The year: I have no idea. Probably 2014.

It was a first kiss from the movies, I tell you. And I'm referring more to the National Lampoon's variety; not some Nicholas Sparks film.

She was a cute little thang. Picture, if you will, a cross between Demi Moore and Miley Cyrus. Weird cross, I know, but that's what she was. Of course, my only comparison is that Moore and Cyrus are both women, one of whom terrifies me, and one of whom doesn't terrify me quite as much. Other than that, I suppose there was very little to compare. In fact, she probably looked nothing like either one of them.

Anyway.

We were on a second date. I invited her over for dinner at my place, which you single people know is code for, *I invited her over to get it on like Donkey Kong.*

Nope. Scratch that… I invited her over to my place for dinner. Period. There was absolutely nothing else on my mind that night. I am as innocent as can be here.

Dinner went as well as it could have gone. I whipped up some amazing shrimp scampi and served it with huckleberry wine and thawed éclairs for dessert. We dined. We laughed. We got along fantastically. We cleaned up the meal mess. We moved to the couch to... you know... talk...

And then it happened.

But before I tell you of our epic "first kiss," let me tell you what I saw sitting in front of me both before and after.

Before: I saw an incredibly beautiful woman. I saw soft skin and beautiful curves. I saw a mind that was so engaging and fascinating to get lost in. I saw eyes that could easily draw you into their eternally satisfying gaze. I saw lips that I wanted to feel pressed against mine. I saw hair that I wanted to run my fingers through to feel its silky magnificence. I saw a person whom I had become so enthralled with, and knew that I would most likely want to see again, and again, and again.

After: I saw Beelzebub, himself; the devil. Mixed with a feral cat. Splashed with the deep and unmistakable desire to run away as fast as my fear could make my legs go.

So, yes. Where were we? We moved to the couch to... talk.

We inched slightly closer to one another as we both pretended we didn't know what was about to go down (pun unintended).

And then, closer.

Soon our legs were touching.

And our hands.

We kept stealing glances at each other's mouths. That's the sign, you know. The sign that you're both done talking. I had been here many times before with many different people. It's definitely one of my favorite moments in the game of... dinner.

I went in for the kiss because society says that's the man's job. The fear I always felt in my youth had long since evaporated. I had learned through trial and error that kissing a girl really isn't very difficult at all. And so I went for it.

Before I got there...

And this is true, my dear readers.

She reached out and grabbed my face fiercely and violently with both hands. The speed with which she did this was chilling at best.

Then she whipped and cranked my head to one side as if she was giving me a chiropractic adjustment.

At this point, I was just confused. It was all happening so fast. I had no idea how to even begin to process this. And I wouldn't need to because what came next would take all the mental processing power I had.

She stuck her tongue out as far as she could push it, which was freakishly far.

And she began aggressively *licking* the side of my face.

What's happening right now?! What's happening right now?! I was paralyzed. I didn't know what was going on enough to figure out how to get out of it. I only knew it was icky and unpleasant.

She wasn't just licking pocket-sized licks, either. She was straight-up beginning at the bottom of my beard, and taking long sweeping swipes up toward my eye.

What?! Huh?! I…. What the… Someone help…

And would you believe me if I told you that her sudden ferocity, or her act of licking, or the shock of it all wasn't the worst part?

The worst part was her tongue itself.

There was no saliva on that thing. It was as dry as a cat's tongue, and twice as rough. It was as if she had attached a piece of fine-grit sandpaper to it, and was attempting to grate her way through to my cheek bones.

It was traumatic for me at best.

I didn't even kiss her. I was an all-taker no-giver that night, and only ever received that wild felineish kiss up the side of my face.

Again.

And again.

And again.

I finally pushed her off playfully and tried to not immediately start wiping her dry-mouthed weirdness away.

"I just wanna take it slow," I told her, calm as a cucumber in a mid-summer heat wave.

I never saw her again after that night.

Profoundly important moral of the story: I'll let you know when I'm done shaking out these chills. Or you can come to your own conclusion. It shouldn't be difficult.

And with that, we'll get back to it...

All the Pretty Ladies

Okay. Let's get semi-serious about love now.

There are five women with whom I learned my greatest life lessons in the following areas: romantic love, that quest to love and be loved by others, the real value of authenticity in relationships, and which dynamics often lead to being really hurt or to really hurting someone else. I absorbed more in my brief time with each of these women than I did in the eight total years I was married.

Tweni, the nickname I gave her, was the first woman with whom I was ever *really* in love. As in, ever. She was also the first woman I asked out for a date after my second divorce was finalized. Believe me. You never want to be a divorcee's first date. You'd have better luck at a successful outcome with a starving crocodile.

I met Tweni at an eating disorder residential rehab clinic graduation party (don't be annoyed at *me* for that ugly little mouthful of words; I didn't name the damned thing). My sister was hosting, and it was the ideal environment for me, the overly-emotional, overly-susceptible, freshly divorced, highly analytical guy to meet a vulnerable, over-sharing, timidly excited about her future, pretty girl.

Tweni was *fantastically* and naturally beautiful even though she didn't always know it. She had bright straight blonde hair that tumbled just below her shoulders. She was tall and slender and graceful. She was kind. Sweetly shy. Trusting. Humble. We laughed together. She loved me with her whole heart. I really believe that. Later, as we parted ways for the final time, she would tell me through heart-broken tears that she had given me the two things she could never get back. Her first love and her virginity.

I never realized just how much those two things meant until I found myself sitting across from her under a pavilion at the city park, pleading with her to choose me instead. She was getting married to some guy she had fallen for after she *finally* found the courage to walk away from me and mean it. Through heavy tears, she looked me in the eyes and said the words, "I don't love you anymore." It was a necessary lie for her to tell. I had promised her that if she could do that, I would leave her alone for good.

During the several months that preceded that moment, I had pushed Tweni out of my life as hard and as fast and as often as I kept pulling her back in. I really *loved* her the way I had never loved a woman before her, and so I could not let her go. I also could not trust that love and so I could not keep her.

She was fresh out of rehab when we met. She had never had a boyfriend or been in love. I couldn't trust that her love for *me* was real. I was freshly divorced. I had ended up marrying the first woman I dated after my first divorce, and that just led to a hot little red head who, for all I know, might have stabbed me in my sleep if she could have gotten away with it; that's how much we disliked each other. And because of all that, I couldn't trust that my love for *Tweni* could be trusted, either.

It wasn't until she walked away, and meant it, that those walls I believed were protecting me came barreling down, leaving my heart dangerously exposed. And, once I realized that she actually was going to go through with marrying the other guy, I finally fought for her.

That's when I knew she was the first woman I had genuinely loved. I never had fought for any other woman in the past. I never felt the agony of having an almost tangible piece of me suddenly disappear the way I did with her. I never cared so deeply for a person that I felt I was losing all the beauty of my future as she turned and walked away. I never felt so strongly for a person that I had no choice *but* to fight for her. I also never loved someone so much that I could somehow see just how badly my actions had hurt her. Through those final tears, my own heart told me that she deserved so much more happiness than I had given her, and it was time to let her go try and have that.

It was with Tweni that I learned just how dangerous it can be to barricade the human heart. I learned that when the right person comes along, love is going to get through those walls anyway. Putting walls up doesn't keep that from happening. All it does is prevent me from being able to properly give my love back in return. It keeps the other person firmly trapped on the outside. It does what it is designed to do; it keeps love from progressing. And eventually, the person on the other side of my walls becomes so tired and hurt from *being* on the other side, that she disappears for good.

Fabulous Mindy was caught in the vortex which followed Tweni. I don't know if I'll ever be at peace with what I put Mindy through. It is an impossible situation to fall in love with someone who is in heavy denial of still being in love with someone else. Fabulous Mindy was in love with me. I was still very much in love with the newly married Tweni. And I *liked* Mindy so much that I wouldn't admit my feelings for Tweni. I didn't want to lose such an amazing new woman as I sorted my heart out.

I called her Fabulous Mindy for a reason. She was fabulous. Gorgeous, head to toe. Like Tweni, she also was a blonde, but she was more of the spicy blonde variety; the kind who always does fancy things to her hair and makes your jaw dangle when you show up on her doorstep. The way her eyes lowered slightly down toward her smile when she looked at you was always so cute to me. She often had this expression when we were together that so clearly said, "I'll love you forever, if you'll just love me in return."

She knew I was in love with Tweni. She could sense it. She would ask me about it sometimes. I would always mosey up to the douche-bar any time she did, and order another shot of heavy denial to keep from hurting her feelings. My emphatic declarations that I was over Tweni would keep her around for a little while, but she always knew. I have no doubt about that. She knew I was comparing everything she and I had together to everything I had with Tweni. She knew I was comparing the fun we had together, the laughs we shared, the adventures, and above all how my heart *felt* in comparison.

The thing was, I *wanted* so badly to love Mindy. I tried to love Mindy. She was everything I could have asked for in a woman. Beautiful. Fun. Easy going. Similar beliefs. Intelligent. A dedicated mother. A hiking companion. A camping mate. My family and friends all loved her. But she was in that nonsensical vortex that followed true love, and she never stood a real chance. Not when every bit of her, and of us, was being compared to something different that, in my mind, was perfection.

I know how badly it hurts to be stuck in that vortex, pinned up next to an immortal of sorts. I was married to a widow on round two, and let me promise you. The dead somehow have a way of becoming perfect when being compared to the living. One can't compete with a dead person. Tweni may have been alive and well, but the situation was no different. She was forever lost to me, and my heart would only let itself remember the good and perfect things that we were together.

I learned so much from those few months I shared with Fabulous Mindy. I learned that for me, it is morally wrong to deny my strong romantic feelings for one person in order to keep a different person from leaving. Mindy was such a strong and good woman, and she didn't deserve that. What I did to her was undeniably wrong. And while I didn't mean to do it to her, and while I didn't want to do it to her, and while I really was trying to force myself to get over Tweni so that I could fall in love with her, a better version of me would have been honest with her, and let her make the decision to stay or go based on the truth.

I also learned with Mindy that I cannot simply force my heart to stop loving someone just because not loving them would be more convenient. Real love doesn't disappear overnight just because the person is suddenly married or because they're gone. In fact, I don't think real love ever disappears at all. I will *always* have a corner of my heart where I keep my love for Tweni tucked away, and I think to some degree I will always still love her.

I am okay with that. The same way I am okay knowing that any person I love now or in the future will have corners in their own hearts forever tucked away for the people they once really loved as well. I will always have a place in my heart tucked away for Fabulous Mindy, too.

I think so much jealousy arises in relationships because we see those lingering pieces of love-now-departed that are forever saddled in the hearts of those we love, and we want them gone, gone, gone. We want them exterminated. We want the people we are currently with to push those others out completely. We want to be their one and only.

Somehow, we fail to see that we *can* be their one and only, and we *can* have their whole hearts, even at the same time parts of their hearts forever remember and feel for those who have come before. If we could just openly admit that it is true for each of us, and also be okay that it is true for those we love, many more relationships would flourish beyond the people of the past. I am convinced of that.

Some time after Mindy came the Farmer's Daughter. It was the nickname I gave to a pretty little brunette with giant green eyes and the cutest pouty lips that would make a man do *anything* she wants. She was a shy firecracker. Don't ask me how that worked, just know that it worked and that I loved it. I've never had as much satisfying fun with someone I've dated as I did with that woman.

A lot of women came and went from my life between Fabulous Mindy and the Farmer's Daughter, and a lot of women since. I went through my man-whore stage during parts of that, where I didn't want to actually love anyone but I did want to get it on with *everyone*.

There was Amanda. She was the six-foot-two West-Coast Swing dancer who I started to really like. After a couple auspicious dates, we had the worst drunk sex imaginable. I am fairly certain one of us fell asleep in the middle of it. She claimed she didn't remember what went down that night (or who), but she disappeared for good after that (minus a quick drop-by to grab some earrings left behind). Amanda taught me that when a dating relationship starts with sex, it better be damned good sex.

There was Sasha. She was the stunning and tiny five-foot-nothin' blog fan who showed up to a local Dancing with the Stars charity event I was participating in. She slipped me her number and met me at a karaoke bar a few nights later. We both were tipsy, we made out at the bar (yes, we were that classy), and that night she taught me what fabulous sex *really* was. It was with Sasha that I learned two things. I learned that with my growing popularity, I could get fans in the sack with little effort. I also learned that it made me feel like a real schmuck when I did. She really liked me, and I took advantage of that and I'm sure I hurt her in the process somewhere.

There was Danika. She was a first year law student who was nice as sugar until it was finals time, then she became mean as nails. Danika had epically perfect augmented breasts of which she always would say, "don't get used to them, I'm getting those suckers yanked out one day." I still laugh about that. We tried dating a couple times but ultimately we couldn't stand each other and decided to try the friendship thing instead. It was with Danika that I learned some people make great friends even though dating is a complete disaster. We are good friends to this day, and I can honestly say that our joint loathing of the times we dated only brings us closer together.

There was Tammy. She was funny as hell and her body would do all these crazy contortionist things that no other woman's body could do because she was a yoga ninja or something like that. The two of us laughed like crazy. I don't think I ever enjoyed a first date as much as I did my first date with her. I had never seen a girl laugh the way she did. I even thought I was falling in love with her after a while. Then I learned that she had been high as a kite during that first date. And every date since. I also learned that she was as crazy and mad as a hornet when she didn't currently have marijuana flowing through her system. I learned with Tammy that who you are authentically is who I will ultimately love or not love. To mask your true self only causes feelings of betrayal and insincerity once the mask comes off, and no lasting relationship can be based on that. I also learned that people who are always high on weed are *always* late.

There was a woman whose name I literally don't know. I have her listed in my phone as "The Catfish." I noticed she was a fan of my blog when I came across her on a dating app. She was passing through town, and would be gone the next day. Texting led to texting, and we decided to have a very innocent and rowdy one-night stand, complete with (according to our texting conversation) pushing each other up against walls, slapping each other's asses with gusto, and the solid follow-up plan to never talk to each other again once it was over. The woman who showed up on my porch a couple hours later was not the woman from the pictures. She was actually not a woman I could usually be attracted to at all. I learned from her that... *Hm.* Let's see. How do I put this? Sometimes it's better to just say goodnight instead of talking yourself into a bad situation that you know will only get worse just to keep from hurting someone's feelings. And it did get worse. Sexual attraction cannot be faked. Sexual regret is real. I know that now.

There was Kendra. Kendra Blue Eyes. Poor Kendra. She showed up during a time of my life where my sexuality got a little confusing to me. Because of that, I couldn't let myself fall for her the way I could have. We became best friends, though. She never judged me or liked me less for who I was and what I was going through. She was an ex-tuba player, just like me, and a hot one. Yeah, how does that happen? She was into Magic cards. And she was gorgeous. How does *that* happen? She also had the bluest eyes I had ever seen on a brunette. One day she showed up on my doorstep and told me she was leaving the next day for Alaska to work things out with her estranged husband. And she did just that. Kendra taught me that a truly good person loves you no matter who you are or what you're going through. I don't know that I'll ever meet another person as accepting of all humans as Kendra was.

After Kendra there were several other women. I was going on two or three dates every week simply because I had nothing better to do on the nights that I didn't have my son.

I learned through all of them that it doesn't matter who I am dating. I click with whom I click with. I fall for whom I fall for. I don't choose the person I love. Love chooses me.

There was Jamie with whom I learned that some people never wear underwear, a fact that was offered up within three minutes of meeting. Fortunately, this person never got a chance to prove it to me.

There was Mary. We went on several dates and I *think* we really liked each other, but she was caught in a different type of vortex: the "I need to be less of a man whore" vortex. She was the first woman I dated after declaring to myself that "I ain't gonna have sex with *anyone* until we've been on at least five dates!" This just led to all sorts of weird dry humping and one confused woman who finally grew tired of it. I learned from Mary that simply stopping frivolous sex cold turkey when one has been having all sorts of fabulous sex of late will lead to nothing but the delivery of pelvic bruises and complete relationship awkwardness. I'm sure her friends snicker to this day when my name is brought up, and I'm probably known now only as "The Rigorous Levi Lover" in their circle.

There was Colette. I learned from her that some people straight-up lie about who they are at the beginning of relationships. She told me she was single, never married, and was a practicing family lawyer. By the end of the date she slipped on her fibs and the truth was *all* revealed that she was a not-yet-divorced mom, mother of three, telemarketer. Once her lies blew up in her face, she threw it out there that she also didn't wear underwear, I suppose hoping it would somehow revive the date. It didn't.

There was Reagan, with whom I learned that some people can go an entire date and never say more than one word in any five-minute span.

There was Taylor. It was on this date I learned that some people literally cannot smell their own overpowering body odor. I may have cried that night the way one cries over a particularly potent onion.

There was Brooke. I learned from her that some women *my* age are already "mothers" to more than six cats. This was almost as remarkable as the fact that she also played the accordion and had it in her car in case I wanted to hear her play. Which I did. And it was a mind-blowing private concert. Be jealous.

There were many others, all of whom taught me about life and about love.

And rarely did I get it on in the bedroom with any of them after Kendra Blue Eyes and before The Farmer's Daughter.

For some reason, something had pulled me hard and fast out of my whorish ways with Kendra. I became much pickier about who I took it off for.

I'm not an idiot. I know that jumping into the sack twelve minutes after meeting someone makes it almost impossible to cultivate any type of real relationship centered on love and respect for one another. I also knew that all that sex wasn't me at all, and I didn't want to turn into one of *those* guys. You know. The kind who literally wants nothing but sex, and arrives at the end of his shortened, sad life, reduced to little more than a walking billboard for gonosyphiherpelaids. I knew I needed to slow the fuck down (pun definitely intended), and so I found a way to do it... Which apparently was to dry hump my way to better habits with whomever came next. Which did and didn't work.

As it turns out, dry humping to stop slutting around is akin to chewing Nicorette Gum to stop smoking. It was a wean to an end. Sorry, Mary. I deserve to be snickered at by more than just your friends for that one. I acknowledge that.

Anyway, besides cutting back on frivolous sex, I decided to try and really date again. I began dating to meet new people. I began dating to find love and to find a partner and a best friend, with sex being an added benefit instead of a driving force. I began dating to find any person who could officially take over the very large part of my heart that still, even that late in the game, seemed to somehow belong to Tweni.

And then I met the Farmer's Daughter.

She didn't just take over my heart. She did it with authority. And after hurting Mindy, I always promised myself that the next woman to own my heart would be the one who walked in and took it away from Tweni, whether I liked it or not.

There was so much to love about the Farmer's Daughter. The way she giggled when she got both nervous and excited at the thought of me sharing a piece of her with hundreds of thousands of people on my blog. Her cute little insecurities that made her pouty lip come out and take over the scene. The way we made plans to watch a movie and would lay in bed irritating each other and wrestling for hours instead. The way she trusted me to do silly things like bench press her or balance on a giant Swiss ball with her on my back. The way she cried when she got drunk on wine. The way we playfully argued with each other about who the boss was in our relationship. The way she fully accepted people who weren't exactly the same as she was. The way we spent hours scrolling between country songs, seeing who could scream out the artist first. The way she loved my son. The way she loved me.

God, I loved that woman.

Don't get me wrong. There are things she did that would have driven me bat shit crazy if I let them. The way she wouldn't say what was really on her mind sometimes for fear that it would sound foolish. The way she wouldn't give me a proper snog when she was wearing freshly applied lip gloss. The way she saw herself as less than beautiful so often. The way she she'd pull out that pouty lip and was never afraid to beat me with it.

Her flaws were ultimately beautiful to me because they were part of who she integrally was. Her flaws also had a way of reminding me that I do plenty of things that could drive her bat shit crazy, too. If she let them. But we loved each other, so we didn't just look past the quirks, and the flaws, and the weirdnesses, but we embraced them and found the deeper beauty that somehow existed in all of them.

I had something incredible with the Farmer's Daughter going. I thought that love would last a lifetime.

It didn't.

Ultimately we had different end goals, and different ideas of how to get there. We both wanted such different outcomes in life when it came down to it, and there never was a good way to mesh those goals into one congruous journey together. We eventually had our tearful goodbye and went our separate ways to listen to our sad country songs alone once more.

A year later I would meet, fall hard for, and allow my entirety to be overwhelmed by one woman. Becky. Becky the dancer. The intellect. The sensationalist. The sensualist. The laugher. The woman so *replete* of what was at times such incredible and other times such destructive wisdom. The gal whom I would ultimately let extinguish so much of what was shining bright inside of me when I met her.

I tried, but the story of Becky, and the vast lessons learned surviving that love, cannot be stuffed into the final paragraphs of one collective chapter such as this, and so right there is where I will leave it.

After Becky, and with a heart still freshly ground into hamburger, came Olivia. She was the last woman I loved deeply (and also lost) as of making my final edits on this chapter which I have been culminating for nearly three years now.

Yes, after Becky was Olivia.

Olivia the emotive. The vulnerable. The hilarious. The sexy. The awe-inspiring. The sweetheart. The empathetic. The giver. She was such a giver. Olivia was saturated in complex goodness. Oh, she wasn't faultless by any stretch of the imagination. But she was so much the opposite of Becky. She loved me for exactly the person I am and never wanted anything but to be loved and admired and to develop as a person alongside me. And even though I was deeply in love with Olivia while we were together, I broke her heart for some fucking reason. I broke it by inventing endless reasons why her love for me couldn't be real, and then finally believing my stupid reasons to the point that I pushed her away and broke things off.

I attempted to write about Olivia, along with the lessons I have learned from that relationship as well. I couldn't do it. That one is still fresh. Too fresh. It all came to an end only weeks ago, as a matter of fact, and book deadlines don't seem to care about fragile or soggy emotions.

No, this chapter's truly scrutinizing glimpses into love-gone-wrong for me must end three years ago on The Farmer's Daughter. My heart cannot handle dissecting more of itself than I have for all of you.

I have only shared what I have thus far because I believe that for so many humans, the pursuit of love is the most difficult part of our existence to be brutally honest with ourselves about. And... hearing someone else's perspective sometimes gives us the unexpected ability to find a little more of our own, so why not share.

Love is a weird thing we so deeply crave and desire and *need*, yet – in it or after it – we rarely allow ourselves to acknowledge the harder self-truths which exist alongside it. Love is full of such hard truths; truths which are obscured by our own insecurities, muddied self-conceptions, our egos, and our need to remain lovable to those we are with, or to those who may one day venture into our paths.

In other words, taking ownership of our half of the shit is the last thing any of us want to do when it comes to relationships because we simultaneously have a need to know that we're always still lovable.

But... *Ugh.*

Those truths are so *fucking* valuable to get cozy with. They shouldn't be feared or disguised or buried. Every one of them is a lesson which, if learned with integrity, will add such richness and passion into our relationships with the *right* people down the road, as well as with the people we have in our lives right now. In every relationship, big or small, lasting or temporary, romantic or platonic, parent or offspring, the invitation to learn life's *most* valuable lessons is always extended to each of us, if we'll just let ourselves go there.

I learned so much from dating each of these women. I learned that I cannot and never will be able to predict the future of any relationship. What beautiful thing I may share with one person today can so easily – and at any point – go down in surprising flames, leaving love behind as only an overly-ripened aftertaste to whatever it was the two of us were once enjoying. I learned that whatever good thing I have going right now – with *anyone* – could last a week, a month, a year, or it could very well last the rest of our lives. There are no guarantees in love. Ever. And being okay with *that* idea sets me free to love without ridiculous boundaries in the times that I do happen into it.

Women. Dating. The need to be loved and the need to give love to others. The desire for true intimacy. The journey to be comfortably known by another person. None of it is a game for me. It is, and always has been, an ongoing and sincere expedition full of bewildering life lessons, extraordinary self-discovery, and deep introspection.

What I have learned over the years about this thing called love, and relationships, and by dating so many pretty ladies, and of sex, and of happiness, and the laughter, and the tears, and of *all* of it really, is this...

Life is ultimately *better* with the right person by my side at night, and life is ultimately *worse* with the wrong person there as well.

Love is not actually the challenge. For me, the true challenges exist in seeking out, finally finding, fully trusting, and holding onto the *right* person amid all the seemingly unending turbulence that life loves to mix into the whole of it.

He thinks the people he dates are disposable. He doesn't appreciate love and he's not willing to work for it when he finds it. He gives up way too easily. He is never satisfied with what he has. He doesn't care who he drags in, and who gets hurt along the way.

To look at my love life from the outside, it would be so natural and easy to come to any of those conclusions. I know this because I have been told all of these things either by family members, friends, and most often by my readers after any relationship comes to an end. How could they not come to such conclusions? I don't really share any of the intimate details of my break-ups. Those particulars are mine, and I have no desire to muck them up and grind them down by passing them around to people who don't have any business knowing them.

The real truth is this. I have – and always have had – sincere hope that I'll one day find my lifelong someone.

I do.

I also believe that only time can confirm to any of us what our futures will look like, whom those futures will include, and whom they will not. The more we try to control our outcomes, the more those thoughts begin to control us.

I have no idea if I will have found love or be with someone when you, dear reader, pick up this book.

I can't predict the future. No person can prognosticate lasting love. All we can do is size up the past, do our best to appreciate and understand the people we love, and make the best decisions we can moving forward. We must learn to appreciate what and who we have by our sides, continually seek out the important things we feel are missing, and *be content* with so much less than perfection, both in ourselves, and in others.

So often we seek for happiness in and through romantic love. I have come to believe this is a great mirage in a vast desert of uncertainty. Happiness is the sweet siren which shows us that which we think we want, and always delivers us something else, far more destructive, altogether.

No, I no longer seek happiness in my quest for love. I seek contentment. I seek to be at peace and fulfilled with so much less than a fairytale. I continually search for the person who will come to understand me, comes to deeply knows my flaws, and then accepts me alongside those flaws and that understanding. I search for that person who will somehow learn not to hide her true self from me, and who trusts me just as fully with her own set of shortcomings. If I can find that person, I know I will be content.

I also do not seek happiness when I am alone. I seek contentment in those times of my life with even more fervor. I continually attempt to understand myself, to come to deeply know my own flaws, and to accept myself alongside those flaws. When I am alone, I search for that version of me who will learn not to hide his true self from himself, and who will trust others with his own set of shortcomings. If I can find that person, I know I will be content.

And if I am content, happiness will simply exist. It will exist automatically and with no further effort on my part, whether it's paired-up with someone or completely on my own.

Granola

And now, one more short and pointless little story from a different time in my life, with an even more pointless moral attached to it, since things got a little heavy there... The year: 1999.

I was home from college visiting Mom and Dad for the weekend.

One morning, I traipsed groggily into the kitchen and enjoyed the most delicious bowl of granola I think I had ever eaten. It was just the right amount of crunch and just the right amount of chewy. There were enough raisins mixed in, but not too many. The slivered almond to whole oat ratio was superb. Mom usually had good quality food on hand. This was no exception.

I'm a bit of a snob when it comes to granola. Call me Goldilocks. If it's not close to perfect, I don't eat it. But when it's just right, I eat whatever is there until it's gone. Damn whoever else wanted some.

Mom always dumped all of her store-bought cereals into large plastic bins made for easy-pouring. There was enough granola left in the bin that morning to fill about four bowls. I had already savagely downed two and was still hungry, so I poured myself a third. I filled the bowl with milk until the top layer of granola barely showed through anymore, and I went to town.

I really wasn't paying much attention to anything. My mind was back at college, thinking about all the women and their lips and breasts and other fun things that I had yet to experience. I don't think I thought a lot about anything else back then.

I sat alone at the large mahogany table in my parents' giant kitchen, and wolfed down bite after bite of that granola, willing my stomach not to fill completely so that I could pour one more fresh bowl and finish it off.

When no more than three spoonfuls remained in the bottom of my dish, I took another scoop and happened to look down at my spoon before I put it in my mouth. There, floating in the milk, was a tiny chubby brown worm, wiggling ever so slightly as it struggled not to drown.

Naturally I dropped the spoon back into my bowl, disgusted. This is when things really got bad.

Floating in my remaining milk was no fewer than eight worms, some of which were dead, some of which were writhing for survival just as the first worm was. My throat tightened and I held my breath. *No. No. No.*

I closed my eyes, reached out, and found the plastic cereal dispenser and pulled it toward me. I certainly didn't want to, but I forced myself to look at it. The sides were semi-opaque. There was no way to clearly see what the contents were.

I pulled it toward me, opened the top, and looked inside. Dozens of tiny worms were attached to the sides, crawling up the container. *No. No. No. No.*

I looked closely at the granola that was still left in the bottom. *No. No. No. No. No. No. No.*

It was *pulsating* with life. Hundreds of tiny brown worms were making their way in and out of the grains and nuts. The cereal was very much alive.

I knew I had only seconds. I slammed the container down and made a run for the bathroom. Just before it all came back up, my entire body seized and my brain took over before I could retch. *If you throw those up, they're going to have to pass through your throat and mouth **again**.*

I had already chewed those little bastards up. I had already swallowed them. They were already dead. And so, I made the impossible decision to keep them down and let my body do with them what it would.

It took me more than a decade to eat another bite of granola after that, and if I'm being honest, I've never enjoyed it to the same degree since.

Pointless moral of the story: check your food to see if it's moving *before* you eat it.

And with that, we'll get back to it…

An Hour to Kill

I had an hour to kill, so I watched him.

From the very back of the Walmart parking lot.

I had a date in the next county over that evening, and an appointment earlier that afternoon I had just come from. I really didn't want to drive back and forth, so I parked my reasonably expensive brand new car at the back of the lot, and cranked the Mumford and Sons Pandora station via Bluetooth from my $900 phone to my 15 different surround-sound Lexus RX350 speakers.

I leaned the seat slightly back to get more comfortable. I cranked up the air. I diddled on my phone. I checked my Facebook. I played some games.

Aside from an old abandoned boat several stalls over, the lot was empty.

Until *he* showed up.

An impossibly old car slowly wheeled in and came to a loud and squeaky halt, six or so empty rows in front of mine. It had nothing but a cracked windshield for windows. The back window and every side window had long ago been replaced by thick, and now rotting, cardboard. Dents and dings lined all sides of it. The paint was chipped beyond recognition. One taillight was non-existent. I couldn't tell the make or model because the emblems had at some point fallen off.

The tires of this unmarked vehicle were worn so thin that they would blow at any moment. A loud explosion from the tailpipe was the textbook final proof that this car belonged in an abandoned field, not in an abandoned parking lot.

The car was directly in front of me. Facing me. For the longest time I couldn't make out any movement. The windshield was so dirty I could only make out the silhouette of a man, sitting so still, seemingly watching me in return.

And then his figure moved slightly.

And I watched him.

His car, which is a title I give loosely to his rolling junk pile, was parked close to the lot exit.

His door opened. Or I should say, after some considerable effort it was opened. It see-sawed back and forth several times as if it was stuck before it finally sprang forward.

Again, there was no movement for some time.

Eventually one foot stepped out to the pavement, with what could have once resembled a sneaker attached to it.

Eventually the other foot appeared.

Why was this man moving *so* slowly? Something about it didn't seem right.

It took him at least two minutes to pull himself up out of his car. And another fifteen to walk around to the passenger side door.

With each eternal shuffle he took, it seemed like hours passed.

He was an old man. Mid-sixties, maybe. Perhaps older. And he was hurting.

Every move he made was hurting him.

Every step he took.

Every turn. Every twist. Every fucking breath of air.

He was moving so slowly because it hurt him *so* much to move.

I know this because I sat. And watched him.

Eventually, he pulled on the handle of the passenger side door. He struggled with it, just as he had with his own. It finally sprang open.

It took him ten more minutes to pull something out of his car. I couldn't tell what it was. It was about the size of a large manila envelope, but thicker. And dirty. And white or brown or... I don't know. I never got a good look at it. I do know that the pain in his eyes could be felt as he retrieved it, even though I was too far away to see them.

With great effort, he closed the door once more.

And he slid a key into the keyhole and locked it. Why, I couldn't guess.

And he held his head as high as his hunched body could.

And he began shuffling.

Toward the corner.

Soon I saw that he had Parkinson's disease. He shook and wobbled, something I hadn't noticed from the distance I was at. But yes, I was almost certain of it, now that it caught my eye.

My watching eye.

I had an hour to kill. An hour to sit. An hour to watch all of this unfold.

It took him no fewer than six hundred shuffled steps, and no less than twenty minutes to reach his intended destination some forty feet away.

His destination on that corner.

That corner of the Walmart parking lot.

And finally I got to see what he was carrying. With great effort, he unfolded... a sign.

He propped himself awkwardly upright against a lamppost.

And he held up his sign. A sign asking for help.

I looked at the clock on my dashboard. *Shoot.* I was supposed to leave two minutes ago.

I revved up my engine.

I put my car in drive.

And I pulled into the exit. That same exit where this man stood hurting, shaking, trying to survive on the corner of a street where I was sitting in my brand new, reasonably expensive car.

I thought about the money I had in my wallet. I had only big bills. Nothing smaller than a twenty. Though I had plenty of them.

I watched him as I waited for the light to turn.

This man.

This emaciated, dirty, dying man…

Shaking.

Trembling.

Wobbling.

Gasping.

Hurting.

And I looked at my clock.

The light in front of me turned green.

And I drove away.

Because… I am not always a good person.

Dan Pearce

Yes. That happened.

All of it.

Did you imagine something more? Did you hope for it, maybe? I'm sorry to let you down, dear reader.

There is no more I can add to this story. Not honestly.

There is no superior ending to share from that particular day and that particular moment of my life.

I did not turn my vehicle around and become the hero you may have expected when you paid for a book meant to entertain or enlighten you.

I didn't suddenly find the compassionate human within to go back, and in some small or profound way alter that man's existence for the better.

Why didn't I?

Because.

I just… didn't.

I am not always a good person.

Why shouldn't that be reason enough?

Those blank pages are brimming with every honest rationalization I came up with. They are filled with each conscience-building lie I told myself and was actually able to believe once I drove away from that parking lot. I never could find any answer that could bring me redemption, and so those pages are empty.

Humaning is hard sometimes.

I actually shared that narrative on my blog. I ended it exactly as I ended it here.

"Because… I am not always a good person." I followed that final line with nothing further because there was nothing further to add.

In my vulnerability, I expected the masses to simply nod their heads and admit that they, too, sometimes didn't do the right thing when presented the opportunity to be better humans.

There certainly were many who did just that. There were far many more readers who became angered, and judgmental, and undignified in their vicious statements attacking my character and morality. The piece went viral, and discussions of my actions took place on social networks as far as the Internet eye could see.

A tiny glimpse into a less-than-perfect moment of my own humanity was being torn to shreds, and two very opposite camps were formed. There was the camp which congratulated my honesty and came to my defense, protected my good name, and fought to keep the destroyers at bay. And on the other side of the field was the camp which cried out, in no uncertain terms, that I was a disgrace to mankind, a heartless and horrible person, and that I most certainly should have done something very different.

Who was correct? Who was wrong? To whom should I listen? Who has the right to shape my future thoughts and actions? Which voices would I let affect my morals and conscience when such opportunities are once again presented? And which would be healthier? To allow the positive or the negative to affect me most?

It is an overly surreal experience to be loved and hated by so many people for the exact same reasons; to be lauded and despised, based on the same common details; to be protected and attacked, all centered around matching particulars.

Try it some time. Nothing will sprout thick pubic-like hair on your ear lobes faster.

I relearned the same lesson that day which I have had to learn again and again since becoming a widely-read writer, and that is this… When it comes to me, and my morality, and my beliefs, and my triumphs, and my struggles, and my shortcomings, and my most human of moments… The fact that so many people so often do hate me and love me for the same reasons is all the proof I need that my opinion of myself is the *only* opinion I should ever care about.

I presented that piece of my life to the masses not to entertain or cause conflict. I shared it for two reasons. First, to hold an integral version of myself answerable to the past. And second, to make myself more accountable to the future.

That moment didn't sit right with *me*. That's all I cared about then. And when I find myself faced with such opportunities or decisions in the future, will I make better choices that sit *more* right with me than that one did? That's all I care about now. I don't give two monkey fucks what you, or my family, or my friends, or my readers, or anyone else thinks. How exactly do the opinions of others have any effect on what I will next believe is right or wrong for *my* life?

To find oneself so bothered by who will think what, about whom, and how harshly or how heralding, is a way of thinking I can no longer grasp. Oh, I can empathize, for sure. The majority of my life was spent in the ever-controlling, always-unsatisfied, constantly fearful shadows of other people's beliefs and opinions. I spent far too much of the one life I have laboring endlessly to live in such a way that I would avoid any and all negative views of me. And do you know what I got for my effort?

Depression. Anxiety. Stress. Trepidation. Hurt. Anguish. Sleepless nights. Self-loathing. Self-hatred. Desperation. Relationships that never should have happened. Relationships ending that never should have ended. And... a whole bunch of people thinking I was such a great guy who was doing A-fucking-okay.

Then one day this "great guy" who was doing "A-fucking-okay" in life almost (and quite purposefully) drove his car off the edge of a cliff. I unbuckled myself. I pointed the nose of my car at the darkness. And I hit the accelerator.

The details don't matter. If you're that curious you can go poking around on my blog and find the entry where I shared it. The only thing that truly matters to me is this: I was at a point where the pressure to be loved and to be perfect had grown so immense, at the same time my desire to have a life finally my own became so overpowering, that I considered *ending* my life a reasonable choice, since I knew I could have one or the other, but never both.

I didn't go over that edge. Instead I made it home, studied my reflection in the bathroom mirror, and as a means to my own survival,

I forced myself to finally look at… *me*. And recognize… *me*. For the first time.

I've shared that moment in great detail. What I have barely shared is one overly powerful awareness that was somehow born in all of it. It was the single realization that forever freed me from caring what others thought, or how they might judge me. And it was so damn simple.

In order to stop caring about all the negative things other people might say or think, I had to *also* stop caring about all the positive things as well.

How was it I had never realized such a simple truth? It was so glaringly obvious!

If I allow the acclamation, praise, and *approval* from others to somehow shape my own views of who I am, and to somehow guide my own perception of just how much value I have as a human, then I will certainly also leave myself open to the opposite. I will be fully susceptible to the disparagement, and vilification, and belittlement from others, as well. One cannot exist without the other, and one *must* exist any time the other is present as well.

In simpler words, to shut all the negative voices out, I had to shut all the positive voices out as well.

And it was *only* when I did this that my life, almost suddenly, became so much more my own.

From there on out, I made it a habit to acknowledge people for their compliments, and then allow myself the thought: *thanks, but I already know who I am*. And, conversely, I made it a habit to smirk at their judgmental statements or negative conclusions about me, and follow up with the same: *thanks, but I already know who I am*.

It took a lot of attentiveness, dedication, and rededication to the task before it became habit. It took a lot of comprehensive reprogramming of my mind. And do you know what I got for my effort?

Self-belief. Strength. Empowerment. The ability to be more intimate. Calmness. Empathy. Compassion. Peace. Contentment.

Happiness. And… a whole bunch of people thinking whatever the hell they wanted about me, and my lifestyle, and my parenting, and my writing, and everything else from my choice to dye my hair and grow it out, to my choice to eat on paper plates.

Sometimes I *am* a fantastic guy who is A-fucking-okay. Sometimes I'm a selfish or apathetic guy who is not okay. Sometimes stress and fatigue get the better of me. Other times I have all the energy and heart in the world to go out into the world, and focus on making other people's lives better.

Life hasn't changed for me when it comes to challenges and triumphs. The struggles of life will come almost as often as the sun rises, and so will the victories, big and small.

What changed was the immense satisfaction I could only feel after the *exclusive* definition of "me" was coming from me, and me alone.

Noah's Shit-Word Spree

The year or so that spanned between thinking I was so famous I could quit my job, and actually learning how to make an income as a blogger can be summed up in three words. Belly-up *broke*.

It was fate, really. Karma had finally come to get me from my teen years when my friends and I would do things like spread fresh dog excrement on the bottom side of a dollar bill, plaster it to the hot sidewalk, and hoot from a distance as people attempted to snatch it up off the ground. One fifty-something woman, caught in the crosshairs of that prank, began dry heaving and fell flat back on her ass after she discovered the poop. I don't know why we thought that was so funny, but I do know that eventually I deserved to struggle with money the way we made her and so many others "struggle" with it on those hot summer afternoons.

During my belly-up broke year, I worked hard. I probably averaged about 70 hours every week trying to get my blog making money and still, I *lost* almost $20,000 that year. That means I was working myself to death for exactly -$5.49 per hour.

Just before I foreclosed on the home I had purchased for nearly $600,000 some seven years earlier, a buyer came in and bought it for $325,000. The short-sale destroyed my nearly perfect credit. My maxed-out credit cards that I was months behind on didn't do much to help, either. To survive that time, I had to sell furniture, my pickup truck, computer and camera equipment, and all sorts of my favorite doodads and gadgets. This is what I remember about that time of my life.

I would wake up in the morning and use less toothpaste than I wanted because a full squirt of it made me stress about the money I would be saving if I could just learn to be happy with less.

I took lukewarm showers and was always sure to keep them to two minutes or less. I'm not sure I ever felt completely clean during that entire year.

I *always* had a headache and the only thing I could pin it on was the stress of being poor. Of course, that wasn't an official diagnosis because I had no health insurance and I would have rolled around in hot coals if it would have saved me a trip to the doctor's office.

I used to lay face down with my cheek to the cold tile in my kitchen because I couldn't afford to run the air conditioner during the summer. One time I fell asleep there, and only woke up when a mouse trap snapped eight feet from my face. I watched as a tiny puff of gray fur flopped wildly back and forth, it's nervous system firing off one last burst of excitement. The mouse died, and I went back to sleep.

For Noah's birthday, I made him a simple cake from a mix that had been sitting in the pantry for God knows how long. Luckily there was some old frosting to go with it. We had no party for him that year. I spent $20 to buy him a birthday present, and felt like I shouldn't eat for the next two weeks to make up for the splurge.

We skipped out on almost everything we were invited to do from camping to eating-out to bowling to picnics. I couldn't admit it was because of money trouble, so I would lie and tell people that I had radio interviews or meetings with book publishers. I don't feel bad about that. If I could go back in time, I would still lie. I would just tell more glorious lies like, "we can't make it because Noah has been invited to be the first child to pet the new baby unicorn in the magical zoo none of you common folk know about."

Belly-up *broke*. I learned a lot from that year spent digging in couch cushions for loose change. More than anything, I learned that having and making no money really just sucks in general. Waking up every morning is not something one looks forward to when you know you're probably going to bed that night with less money and more stress than when your feet first hit the floor. Sure, there is fun to be had here and there, but it was always shadowed by the fear of what that fun was costing me both in money and in time.

Deep into that year and not having any idea when we'd finally find our feet again or if I could even keep doing it much longer at all, Noah and I were sitting at the kitchen bar coloring pictures of monsters together.

"I don't need this shit!" he suddenly exclaimed, as he colored wings onto his bright blue and green scaly creation.

"What'd you say?" My eyes immediately went from overly-tired to projecting from their sockets.

His emotions didn't change. He just kept looking at his paper, scribbling something amazing with his ever-dulling crayon. "I saaaiiiid, I don't need this shit!"

I will confess that I'd never really thought through how I would handle such a moment when it happened, and I somewhat panicked. Where had he *heard* that phrase? I had never turned on anything more than a PG movie for him, and as far as I knew, he'd never heard me cuss. Okay, I lied. One time I accidentally stabbed myself in the wrist with a screwdriver and yelled "hotdammamamma," but other than that, I knew I had been pretty careful about what I let slip around him. I knew that he certainly didn't learn that phrase at Dad's house.

"Where'd you hear that?" I asked in an apathetic tone, not wanting him to feel bad for something he didn't yet understand was wrong, but more importantly wanting him to not feel like whoever he was about to rat out would be in trouble for it.

"Avatar."

Are you fucking kidding me? Avatar? You're three. My thoughts started racing. The stresses of life began bubbling hard and fast against the new stimuli that I really didn't want at the moment.

I quickly ducked into the next room, called his mom right then and there, and had one of those "what are you letting our kid watch over there?!" discussions. I *may* have blown it a little bit out of proportion. Okay, I blew it way out of proportion. His mom felt bad, not having realized how un-kid-friendly Avatar might just be. She thought he'd just pay attention to the cool blue people and not the murder and the cursing and the weird nippleless boobies attached to those cool blue people.

After a short but intense discussion, we worked it out. I snapped shut my phone as I walked back into the kitchen and looked at Noah. It was time to give him "the speech" about using grown-up words at such a young age.

Before I could give it, he said it again. "We don't need this shit, Dad!"

I reached up and pushed against my always aching temples. "Okay. Noah, that's a word we don't use in this house."

"What word?"

"Shit."

I felt so dirty saying it to my kid, but how do you not in such teaching situations?

"Shit?" he chimed back.

Ugh.

"Yep. Don't say that word."

"Shit. Shit. Shit. Shit. Shit. Shit. Shit..."

"Noah, what did I *just* say?!"

"Shit. Shit. Shit. Shit. Shit. Why can't I say shit, Dad?"

I groaned. I was not enjoying this parenthood moment. "Noah, I'll tell you why it's a grown-up word, but when I ask you not to say something you don't say it anymore, okay?"

"Okay."

"Thank you."

"I won't say shit, Dad."

I smiled at the irony. "Thank you."

"Can you say shit?" He looked at me with those giant eyes of his, as if he had no clue what tricks he was pulling.

"Noah, stop saying shit. Do you need an uh-oh?" I did my best to glare him down. I had only enough energy to fight away the funniness of it, or to be stern about it, but not both, and he knew it.

"But you just said shit."

This kid is too smart for his own good.

I watched him for a long moment. "I'm sorry, you're right. I shouldn't have said it. Let's both try not to say it until you're older. Okay?"

"How come?"

"Because it's a grown-up word."

"How come it's a grown-up word?"

I didn't really know. "It just is. It's a word we don't say in this house, okay?"

The corners of his mouth tightened upwards. "What does shit mean?"

"Noah... don't say that again."

"Sorry."

"Thanks, buddy. I know you don't know that some words are not good, but when you find out that some words are naughty you shouldn't..."

"Shit! Shit! Shit! Shit!"

I sighed, only to cover up the building need to laugh that I was now fighting. "Go have an uh-oh."

He sulked off of his barstool and headed for the kitchen wall. "Dad, I *promise* I won't do it again."

"You made an interesting choice to say it again. You still get an uh-oh."

He leaned his head against the wall and stared at the ground. I reached across for the egg timer and set it to four minutes. Before I could set it back down, I heard him mumble. "I don't need this shit."

I started laughing.

He turned and looked up at me with a mischievous grin spread across his cheeks.

"I don't need this shit, Dad!"

My laughing intensified. "Noah!" I screeched, irritated at myself for not controlling my amusement.

"I don't need this shit! I don't need this shit! Dad, we don't need this SHIT!"

I wanted so badly to correct him, but at that point I developed a serious case of the laughing fits, and the more I tried to contain them the worse they got. Noah took this as permission to start yelling the word repeatedly and without end.

"SHIT! SHIT! SHIT! SHIT! SHIT!"

I finally managed to get the words out between laughs. "Noah... [laugh] you... [laugh] just... [laugh] got... [laugh]
more... [laugh] [laugh] [laugh] time... [laugh] added... [laugh] on."

"But Dad, you were laughing at it and you shouldn't laugh at stuff that's bad!" he said.

This only made me laugh harder. I was out of control at this point. I couldn't say anything. The back of my head started pulsating with pain the laughing was so bad.

"SHIT! SHIT! SHIT! SHIT! SHIT! SHIT! SHIT!"

I just shook my head with desperate tearful eyes, unable to speak. He began laughing almost as hard as I was, and soon found himself overtaken by a laughing fit of his own.

I didn't know what to do. He obviously felt that repeatedly dropping the S-bomb was thoroughly entertaining me. It clearly was entertaining him to the point that any punishment was very much worth it to him. And I knew that it was my fault that a mixed message was being given. But geez. When you get the laughing fits, there's not a whole lot you can do to stop them.

I finally locked myself into the bathroom until it was under control. I looked in the mirror and surveyed myself as I regained my composure. My cheeks were tear-stained from all of the laughing.

I bit my lip and opened the door. Noah was still giggling. I used every bit of super human strength I had to keep from laughing again.

It didn't work. And back into the bathroom I went. I got it half-way under control, and when I came back out I told him, "Noah, here's the deal. You still gotta do your uh-oh and we're gonna start the time right now. But I want you to promise me you won't say that word again, okay?"

"Okay, Dad," he said still giggling.

He looked at me with those giant eyes. I could tell that he was dying to say it again. He was trying so hard not to. But he wanted to see me laughing again. *Don't do it.* He *needed* to see me laughing again. *Don't do it!*

The suppressed laughter was pushing full-force against the back of my throat.

His eyes got unbelievably bigger.

The corners of his lips curled up even higher.

His nose scrunched to a tiny point.

Don't. You. Dare.

"Shit."

That's when I *truly* understood the term rolling on the floor, laughing out loud. And to be honest, I don't remember a lot of what happened after that.

I do remember the lessons I learned that day.

I learned that semi-innocently swearing kids can be *really* funny.

I learned that the human body can physiologically only handle so much stress before it *will* break and find some way to release some of the pressure. Usually that is going to be through tears, whether by laughing or crying. I also learned that if we don't do what is necessary to relieve that stress when we feel it building, we will probably not get to choose when that stress gets relieved.

I also learned that sometimes we really need to experience moments like this one to reset us. Something about Noah's shit-word spree and the hard laughter that ensued for both of us was therapeutic. It made me feel like I *could* keep going. It made me realize that Noah's words were true. "We don't need this shit, Dad!"

More than anything, I learned that when we find it difficult to find those reasons to laugh, our kids will always make it possible if we can see past the immediate need to parent, and just let them do their job.

Stacking Quarters

After more than four hours of uninterrupted standing, my knees became increasingly wobbly beneath me. In that dark hallway, with my face firmly pushed against the cold hard wall, my heart never once slowed. The pressure to tell what only I knew was building. I had to admit my involvement in what had happened if this was ever going to end. It was now 1:51 AM.

I looked over at Eric. I had gotten my brother into this mess. His own face was pressed against the wall just as mine was. His hollow eyes stared back at me with a look of despair. He couldn't last much longer. I could sense that he was getting close to cracking. What he would tell them if he did, I couldn't guess. He didn't know of my involvement, and he had nothing to do with what had happened.

Kneeling between the two of us was Amy, her face pressed into the wall just as ours were. Her legs had gone out long before, and she had slumped into a miserable little pile on the ground between her two older brothers. She had cried several times since we were forced there. Her tears were not resting easily on my conscience.

To Eric's right was Tomi Ann, the oldest of our sibling group. She had avoided eye contact with all of us for the most part. At one point, an hour earlier, our eyes had locked and I recognized in that one brief moment that she knew it was me. How could she not? It was *always* me that got us into these messes.

"All you have to do is tell us who did it, and we'll let you all go," the voice came from behind us. It was heavy and haunting. I took a deep breath and bit my lip to calm my racing blood. I couldn't tell them. Not yet. If I held off long enough, we just might all get out of this, unscathed. "Suit yourself," the voice said once more. The shadow that belonged to the voice disappeared behind its owner and we were left in dark isolation to suffer, and to think as a group.

As soon as we were alone again, all three of my siblings visually drooped. "Who did it? Just tell them so the rest of us can get out of here," Tomi Ann pleaded. Eric said nothing. Amy began sniffling below us once again.

I replayed my crime over and over in my mind. There was no way I could confess. No possible way. Sure, my siblings would be free, but I would most certainly be dead for what I had done. My gut told me that as long as I held out, this would be as bad as it got. They wouldn't hold us forever. Of course, one hour had turned to two, two to three, and now here we were, four hours later and there was no end to our suffering in sight.

Finally, when Tomi Ann had stopped her begging, and Eric had dropped to his own knees, and Amy had simply gone silent, I did what I had to do and I threw my little sister under the proverbial bus. I asked her to sacrifice herself, so that I could keep living. They wouldn't kill her. They *would* kill me. I hadn't taken the money. But I had *done* things with the money that were unforgivable.

"Amy, if you tell them you stacked the quarters, I'll give you my lunch box," I whispered. "Then they'll let us go. You'll get in less trouble than the rest of us because you're so little."

My lunch box seemed a suitable trade for my own life. I was, after all, the one who stacked the quarters that day.

In Dad's bedroom closet, he kept a large bowl full of loose change. Earlier that afternoon, I had entered his closet to put a pair of his shoes where they belonged as I set about finishing my daily chores. A brand new roll of quarters sat against the edge of the bowl, unopened. In large blue font on each side, it read $10.

I was in second grade at the time. We had just learned in school that there were four quarters in every dollar, and so this roll of quarters utterly fascinated me. I quickly attempted to do the math in my head when I saw the dollar sign. *Ten dollars, ten dollars, let's see, that would be how many quarters?* I hadn't learned my times tables yet, so I decided to see for myself. I ripped open the roll and stacked the quarters into ten perfect stacks on the shelf next to Dad's bowl of change. Satisfied, I left them all there and went about my business.

Dad found them just before our bed time that night, and that's when all hell broke loose.

"Who's been in my closet?" It boomed through the house as I brushed my mouth full of baby teeth, missing teeth, and my new giant and awkward grown-up beaver teeth. My gut attempted to swallow itself as I remembered the ten stacks of quarters I had left there. "All you kids get in here. RIGHT. NOW!" the voice was coming from my parents' bedroom.

When Dad yelled like that, you didn't even think about it. You obeyed. I hastily spit my toothpaste out and wiped the foamy corners of my mouth onto the sleeve of my thinning Transformers pajamas. By the time I got to the hallway, Tomi Ann and Eric were already there. Amy wasn't far behind. We all marched together into his room where we were greeted by Dad and Mom, standing side by side.

Dad had his hands placed firmly on his hips, a chilling look spread across his face. Mom had one eyebrow slightly raised, her lips pierced tightly together.

"Who was in my closet today?" Dad rumbled at the group.

All three of my siblings immediately shook their heads. Tomi blurted out, "not me! I promise!" I added my own adamant denial into the chaos.

"Who went into my closet and stacked the quarters?" Dad demanded, taking a menacing step toward us.

We all stood motionless, none of us saying anything this time. I swallowed hard, praying he wouldn't call me out for it. Dad didn't say another word and marched past us toward his closet. "Get in here," he said. We obeyed. He proceeded to show us the ten stacks of quarters and again asked who was responsible. Again all four of us pled our innocence.

"Out!" he ordered. We all exited the closet.

Now Mom jumped in. "Just tell us who stacked the quarters. We know you didn't steal any of them. We just want to know who stacked them."

We all stared back with big eyes. I looked over at their dresser. The Smashball paddle was in easy arm's reach. I certainly wasn't going to admit to this thing. I'd get a heavy whoopin' on the bare cheeks for sure.

After another five minutes of back and forth, Dad told us all that if one of us wouldn't admit it, we'd all be punished until whoever did it finally confessed. When the threat didn't get him what he wanted, he sent us all out into the hallway to put our noses against the wall until the truth surfaced.

"Amy, if you tell them you stacked the quarters, I'll give you my lunch box," I whispered some four hours later. "Then they'll let us go. You'll get in less trouble than the rest of us because you're so little."

"No!" she replied. "I didn't do it."

"Come on. I'll give you my globe, too." I knew she had been jealous of my globe ever since I scored it at the neighbor's garage sale for twenty cents.

I loved that globe. It was the first thing I remember really wanting and buying with my very own money. Even at a young age, it fascinated me to realize how small and insignificant I was compared to the vastly huge world. Four-year-old Amy used to love coming in my room and spinning the thing, which is why I was surprised when she turned that down, too.

The older and wiser Tomi Ann finally chirped in. "Danny, it's obvious you did it or you wouldn't be offering to give her your stuff. Just admit it so we can go to bed."

I scoffed. "I'm just tired and wanna go to sleep. I didn't do it." She scoffed back and I turned my attention back to Amy. The wheels in her head were turning. I just needed to sweeten the deal a little more and I'd be out of this for good. "Amy, I'll give you my desk, too. So if you admit it you get my lunch box, my globe, and my desk."

Cha-ching.

If there was one thing she longed to have more than my globe, it was my desk. Being the fourth child, she was stuck in a life of waiting for the next kid up to grow too big or to grow too old for whatever it was she wanted. I had gotten the desk from Tomi Ann. Eric would get it from me. Amy knew she wouldn't see it against her wall for a few very long years at best.

She repeated the deal back to me five or six times to make sure she understood exactly what she'd be getting in exchange for falling on the sword. Eventually Eric groaned and said, "Amy, just do it, that's a lot of good stuff."

"Fine," she said.

I again swallowed heavily as she pulled her face off of the wall, stood up, and made her way around the corner and into Mom and Dad's bedroom.

Would she rat me out? Would she tell them that I had bribed her? Would this really be the end of it?

I tried to listen-in. The only thing that made it back to where the three of us remained were quiet mumbles. I heard no yelling or anger. A few minutes later, Amy emerged followed by Mom and Dad. "Go ahead, Amy," Mom urged.

"I'm sorry I lied and you all had to get in trouble," she squeaked. A rush of relief spread over me. My heart finally slowed. I was off the hook. It had worked.

"Amy told us it was her," Mom said.

"I hope you all learned a lesson. All of you go to bed now," Dad said.

We happily did so.

My family still laughs about this night around the dinner table from time to time some 27 years later. Each one of us has our own version of what happened. My three siblings and I are convinced that we were on that wall until two in the morning. Mom and Dad swear they never showed any anger, and that it wasn't nearly that late nor did the punishment last nearly that long. I suppose in the end what matters is the lessons we each learned.

I learned very different lessons at the time than what I learned later on in life as a father myself.

What I learned in the moment and in the days that followed was very counter-productive to what Mom and Dad were attempting to teach us.

I learned that it wasn't all that difficult to take advantage of the innocent. I bribed Amy into taking the hit for us all, and then I coerced her into giving all of my stuff back a few days later. That was a dangerous lesson to learn.

I also learned that withholding the truth for long enough would probably give me enough time to find a way around it. From that day forth, dishonesty and secrecy became my forte in that home.

I understand the lesson that was trying to be taught. I understand that they wanted to *show* us all that dishonesty can hurt more people than yourself. They wanted to teach us that honesty up front could save us all sorts of long-term negative consequences. But that lesson was lost on me because the fear I had of the consequences of dishonesty outweighed all of it.

Once Noah reached the age where I had to start giving him punishments for poor choices, I found myself thinking back to that night on the wall and the lessons I learned.

I stacked a roll of quarters into ten even stacks. That's all I did. I didn't steal any of them. I just piled them up. So why was admitting the truth of something so negligible such a terrifying notion to me?

The honest truth is that I don't remember enough of the reasons why I was usually disciplined as a child to give you a very good answer. What I do know is that I never had a proper belief that the punishment would fit the crime. I believed I would be punished swiftly, mightily, and equally for the smallest infractions to the biggest ones, and so I treated every mistake I ever made as equal.

Now that I have a son of my own, I sometimes gauge whether or not he fears me the way I feared my own parents when I was little. I understand that if my child will not confess menial things because he is not confident in my ability to keep from overreacting, then I need to rethink things both as a dad and as a disciplinarian.

As my kid gets older, my role in his life is going to change. His mistakes will become more his business and so much less my own. He will start taking his own big lessons away from his actions. As he does, he needs to know that he can come to me and confide his mistakes in me. He needs to know that he can ask me for my advice. He needs to know that he can say, "Dad, I did something kind of stupid," and that I'll help him know how to handle it without blowing things out of proportion.

Looking back at this, I really believe that right now is when I am earning the trust of the future young adult version of my son. Every reaction I have is going to clump together to determine just how safe he feels being imperfect in my eyes down the road. I just hope I get enough of my reactions right that my kid wants his old man's advice for life.

About Time

"One! Two! *Wait!*" I holler at Noah as I use every muscle in my core to keep from flopping heavily on top of him. "Wait 'till I say three!"

"Okay, okay, I'm trying to go at the right time, Dad!" he chimes back as he hops down from the giant stability ball I'm currently balancing on and climbs back up onto the couch next to me.

I find my balance once more and reiterate the instructions. We are attempting a new balancing trick to add to our ever-growing repertoire. This one involves Noah leaping from the couch and planting his feet on the right side of the ball at the exact moment that I lean left to counterbalance him. The plan is for him to then pull himself up onto me and carefully stand up. Once he's precariously planted there, we both will put our arms up and yell, "ta-da!" It's a bit daring, a bit dangerous, and really fun. If he jumps too soon, it pulls me and the ball on top of him. If he jumps too late, he gets a faceful of rubber and I end up ass first on the floor.

"Okay, now wait until I say three to jump this time."

"Okay."

"One." He squats.

"Two." He jumps.

"Wait! I didn't say three yet!" I yell as I fall heavily to the floor. "Wait till I say three!"

It would take another thirteen attempts before we nail it. We then immediately do it correctly no fewer than eight times in a row, and we eventually get bored and start planning a new trick, the amazingness level of which has never before been seen by mankind.

Other times I'll balance myself on the ball and he'll have free reign to climb on and latch himself down however he likes. We then see how long we can balance on it while jumping, and rocking, and just kind of going crazy in general.

It always ends in either gut-grabbing laughter or tears. There is no middle ground. It's one of the reasons we love doing it.

The next day I find myself angrily staring Noah down. "Put it back," I tell him, scowling as fiercely as I can.

"No!" he says between laughs, proud of himself for how far off of the Chutes and Ladders board he just flicked my player.

"Put it back, or I will do something you're not gonna like." I raise one eyebrow and with one hard look, I dare him to try me.

"Go ahead. I'm not getting your dumb piece," he says, pretending to be a smug little snot. He *wants* to see what I'm plotting for my revenge.

With that, I lunge forward and grab him. I've been saving up for this. I pin his body between my legs and let one rip. He starts squealing in horror. "I warned you," I say.

He immediately jumps up and starts squawking as if he's deeply affected by my actions. I turn my attention away for no longer than a moment, and he immediately leaps forward and sits on my face. "I'm gonna sit here until the biggest one in the whole world comes," he tells me.

We horse around for another five minutes at least before we continue our board game.

That night it's his last night at Dad's house before he heads over to his Mom's place again. "What do you want?" I ask him. "A book or a story?" He chooses a story just like he always does. He likes the stories I invent for him.

He races to my bed and insists that we turn off every light in the house before I begin. For some reason he likes it pitch black. Once that task is finished, I climb between the covers next to him and I proceed to tell him the most magnificent story I've come up with yet.

This one is about a little mouse who lived on a giant ship all by himself. The ship never went anywhere, it just sat at the port getting old, and mossy, and worn down.

One day the mouse decided to have some friends over to try and make life a little less boring, but there was a problem. He didn't have any friends. They had all moved away or they had drifted apart. So he made his way down the mooring line and set out on a quest to find new ones.

The mouse's name was Noah. I always let Noah choose the names of the characters. Noah is always the name of the main character. That is, until he realizes that in any particular story the main character is a bad guy, then I have to change it.

And in this story, the mouse named Noah runs down the mooring line and begins his search for new friends.

He starts at a nearby pub. A fat mouse is sitting outside on a wicker chair, brushing his whiskers. "I don't have any friends," Noah tells him. "Will you be my friend?" The fat mouse turns him down and tells him he has better things to do than to hang out with skinny little loners.

But Noah doesn't let it get him down. He knows others are only mean because they don't like something about themselves. The fat mouse was probably pretty sad that he was fat, and he was going to take it out on anyone who tried to be nice to him.

Next Noah tries the bakery. A small shaggy dog is lounging lazily by the door. Noah asks him if he wants to be his friend. "Dogs aren't friends with mice," the dog retorts snobbishly. "Come back when you can play fetch and howl at the moon like I can," he says.

Noah doesn't get discouraged. He knows the dog is probably just having a hard day, and so he continues his quest.

Story time often lasts for an hour or more, never intentionally. The mouse *has* to find his new friends before it can end, but I can't just make it easy for him. That mouse needs to learn some valuable lessons about others and why they act the way they act, first.

He tries a rat. And a raccoon. And a ferret. And a squirrel. They all turn him down.

Eventually he happens upon a giant orange sleeping cat who he's understandably terrified of at first glance. He starts to tip-toe by, and as he does so, he pauses and watches her for a moment. He realizes that he's never actually *met* a cat. He's only been told that all cats are mean and that he should stay away from them all. Something tells him, not all cats are the same and he shouldn't judge this cat before he meets her.

He cautiously nudges the cat awake, and asks her to be his friend. "I've never had a real friend," the cat replies. "You're a mouse and I'm a cat. Doesn't that scare you?"

"Are you going to eat me?" Noah says.

The cat thinks for a moment. "No, not if we're friends."

"Good," Noah replies. "I don't care what other people think. Let's be friends anyway."

The cat agrees, and together they find even more friends and they all go have a party on the boat. Even the first fat mouse eventually shows up and asks to join them.

By the end of the story, Noah is hugging tight to my arm. He likes happy endings.

A few minutes later, I'm tucking him into his own bed, singing him a song about poop-corn and pee pie.

As I pick up the clutter from around the house before heading to bed a few hours later, I come across his iPad sitting in the middle of the living room floor, and I smile.

He was playing with it the day before when I first asked him if he wanted to practice some exercise ball tricks. He loves that iPad. He's got hundreds of games and videos and learning programs on it. He could easily spend his entire day on that thing, yet the *moment* I asked if he wanted to play with me, he tossed it aside and screamed with excitement.

As I pick up the device and place it onto the charger, I am reminded of a lesson I have learned again and again since becoming a dad. There is *nothing* my son craves more than quality time spent laughing and learning with his father.

My son's room is full of expensive toys and gadgets. He's got remote control helicopters and Lego sets galore. He's got an iPod, an iPad, and his own computer. He's got robot bugs and Transformers, super hero action figures and light sabers. And still, there isn't a thing he owns that he doesn't immediately and happily toss aside when Dad walks into the room and invites him to play.

I live my professional life around technology. It's why he has the iPad and the computer and many of the other gadgets he does. He is the lucky only child of a Dad who often upgrades to bigger and better things, and who then passes down his stuff to the only one who's there to take it.

I've often thought about whether or not it is healthy and okay for him to have all that stuff. The last thing I want is to raise a spoiled little brat.

As a parent, I don't have all the answers of what is right and wrong. I don't think that much of anything is ever universally right and wrong when it comes to parenting. What I can honestly say is this. I don't believe there is anything wrong with a child having lots of things. I believe the problems arise and exist when things are used to raise the child.

In other words, parents who get their children stuff and use the stuff to keep from actually having to parent are probably going to have shitty kids.

Parents who know that their kids will want and remember the fun and all of the quality time, far more than they will want and remember the things we can buy them, will probably have awesome kids. So long as they set aside plenty of time to give that to them.

I've learned that there really is no perfect way to parent. There is no magic formula. Am I there in my kid's life? Do I take the time to teach my kid? Do I do my best to be the kind of adult I'd like them to someday be? Do I apologize when I make a bone-headed parent move?

Do I genuinely cherish my kid, faults and all? If so, then I'll be all right. My kid will turn out all right.

I know because I make a *lot* of bone-headed moves as I raise my kid, and he's still turning out pretty damn good.

Conclusion: Waking Up

As I scan through the admittedly dusty annals I call my memory, I can very specifically remember scores of different nights in which I lay awake late into the wee hours of the morning, *thinking*.

I would repeatedly kick the covers off in frustration and later pull them back on again. I would shuffle from my front to my back, and from side to side. I would groan every time I looked over at the clock and see the hours advancing. Some of those nights I couldn't sleep because of excitement. Others because of anxiety or fear. Others because of guilt, sadness, or tormenting myself about the unknown. Sometimes, it was simply the anticipation of something to come.

As I think back and try to list the *mornings* in which I lay in bed full of emotion, only five come to mind.

On three of those mornings, I was angry and quite literally murderous. I would reach up and thrash at the air every so often. I would yell out harshly. I would cover my face with a pillow and pray for Death to somehow arrive and take my most recent tormentor with him. I would usually curse aloud, repeatedly. I was not my usual self those three mornings, and *how could I be* when some damned housefly was continually landing on my face, making it impossible to sleep? You know what I'm talking about. And you know you become just as angry and murderous as I always do.

But in all seriousness, there were two mornings on which I awoke and could not make myself get out of bed for what seemed like the entire day. Both mornings I simply lay flat on my back, motionless, staring up at the ceiling above. *Thinking.*

The first morning was the day after my second wife unexpectedly, but expectedly, loaded-up and took off.

I felt as if a hundred-pound sack of steel marbles was planted squarely in the middle of my chest. Every failure of my life, and there were *so* many, haunted me in that moment. I was thirty, and I would be divorced *twice.* I didn't know how that had happened. That had never been in my life plan.

As I lay there, I thought through every major aspect of my existence. I thought of whom I was to others, whom I actually was, and of whom I wished that I could openly be. And then a funny thing happened.

The sum of it all made me realize just how much I had been *struggling* to live a life that wasn't actually my life at all. I realized in that moment that I would continue to fail repeatedly, and *forever,* so long as I kept attempting to be exactly the man whom others expected me to be; so long as I kept doing exactly what others expected me to do. It was an equation that wasn't working, had never worked, and that would *never* work.

My life wasn't failing because of some lack of effort or skill. It was failing because it wasn't my life at all. It belonged to my parents, my friends, my neighbors, my colleagues, my siblings. This was all a momentous realization for me. And it was a consuming one, as well.

This enlightenment didn't charge me up, or excite me, or motivate me to change things. If anything it depressed the hell out of me for some time. With a realization like that, there are really only two things I could do next, and neither of them left me feeling hopeful.

I could accept that my life wasn't my life, and continue living that inauthentic life. While I would never be happy, this would definitely be the easier route to take. I would never lose many of my family and friends if I took that path. I could somehow still find a way to maintain the respect and admiration of others, throughout each and every failure that would come my way. It would be miserable, but it would be livable.

Or I could do an impossibly harder thing, and I could jam a flag into the cold powdery hilltop of my own existence, and declare that it now belongs to *me*. To do so would alienate me for sure. It would scare others. It would push many away. If this wasn't true, *everyone* would live an authentic life, free from the judgments and voices of others.

In the days and weeks after my wife split, anyone who came across me could feel the sadness oozing from me. I let them just believe that I was sad over the demise of my marriage. I honestly didn't care all too much about that, but I was thankful for the timing because it let me be sad and pensive about my own life in a time when I really needed it. I think sometimes because we want to appear as nothing but happy and positive and strong to others, we don't properly give ourselves those moments of penetrating reflection.

Yet it is in moments such as those that the real greatness of life is so often born. It certainly was for me. I just didn't know it yet. It actually had to get much worse before it could get better. I had to let the awareness of inauthenticity fester so freely that it would eventually became dangerous and unsurvivable.

Two and a half years later, in overwhelming despair, I nearly drove my car off that cliff.

I didn't go over the edge. I somehow survived those thoughts when they were at their darkest.

And from there, I went home, studied my reflection, and *found* a way to change the way I viewed just about everything. I did so immediately and without any fear for what would follow.

There was something about the ridiculousness of it all that shook me to a place of committed action. I clearly remember laughing to myself at one point, shaking my head, and saying aloud: "Holy shit. You *honestly* thought driving off a cliff was better than a few people thinking you're messed up?! Geez, man. Stupid much?"

Deep exhale.

Laugh.

Friends and readers, as tangible as it all was to me for so many years... It really was ridiculous. Every bit of it. The entire culture of never-ending pressure that we place on each other is bizarre. And ludicrous. And preposterous. And straight-up absurd.

And *that* was what suddenly became so clear to me. It was so clear, in fact, that it became a completely laughable notion almost overnight.

A short time after that dark moment in my car, I found myself fully-awake one fall morning, once again staring at the ceiling from my bed, just as I had the morning after my second marriage ended. Only this was *very* different.

I don't remember what I thought throughout most of the morning, though. I only remember what I felt.

It was *pure* happiness.

Happiness by itself is one thing to feel. Pure happiness is something else altogether.

I felt happiness throughout my entire life, and often. I felt it when I unexpectedly made extra money, or when I first held Roxy as a new puppy. I *really* felt it the day I became a Dad, and I felt it the day the vending machine gave me two candy bars instead of one. Hell, I even felt it in more selfish moments like when my nemesis at work got busted for lying to clients, or when I bumped into one of the most popular and vicious girls in high school and saw that she had gained a hundred pounds. I know I probably shouldn't have, but I felt happiness in those moments, too.

But it wasn't until that fall morning, smiling and staring at my ceiling, that I felt *pure* happiness.

Pure happiness, like real love, is one of those things you don't know you've never experienced until the day you finally do.

In that single moment, it hits you that your life is your life, your happiness is your happiness, and your next move is all your own. You feel no effect at the thought of having no money or having a lot of it. You feel no effect thinking about what others believe and what they tell you that you should believe. You know what you believe and you are okay if it is different. In that cumulative moment, you also feel no effect at the thought of what others might think of you for any decision you will make next.

Pure happiness is a great moment of freedom, and it is also a great moment of independence. In that same single moment, you cannot think a judgmental thought about another human. You don't wish bad fortune on even the biggest assholes in your life. You are strangely okay with anyone else believing what they want to believe and doing what they want to do with their own lives.

You realize in that moment, more than you ever have before, that other people's lives are their own, and you don't need to have a say in *anything*. Perhaps that thought scares some people, but I promise you that when you genuinely feel it, it is incredible.

My life's first moment of pure happiness, the morning I lay awake in that bed, was in the days after I acknowledged the most difficult of my self-truths which finally freed me to be who I always knew I was.

But that wasn't what actually did it. It was just the final piece to a much larger puzzle that I had been working endlessly on for years. These self-truths were simply my last existing demons that needed exorcizing, and they were the concluding act I had to perform in order to take full ownership of my own life.

During the time that things had gotten harder and darker, I had done a *lot* between that moment of pure happiness and the sad morning, years earlier as I lay awake, wishing to disappear from being.

During that time, I made my beliefs my own by declaring that I believed and always had believed something different. I made my sexuality my own by admitting it to myself and then admitting it to others. I made my relationships my own by deciding what *I* thought was right and wrong when it came to sex and marriage and everything in between. I made my conscience my own by admitting and righting many of my past wrongs. I learned to metaphorically flip the bird to all the online haters, and to stop letting their venomous actions affect me so deeply. I made my self-worth my own by writing about and confronting the bullying from my past. I made my body my own by learning to accept its imperfections while falling in love with the quest for better health.

It took time, and it took tears, but I took my life and I made it authentic. My life was my life. Every glorious moment and every mistake. Every moment of inspiration and every moment of stupidity. The freedom to own all of it and to be okay with *all* of it… *that* was pure happiness.

And that's all this book is about. It is about the ability we each have to finally *own* an authentic life.

I spent so much of mine running from most of the stories that I shared with you in these pages. I wasted so many years pretending that I was never bullied, and that the bullying had no long-term effects on me. I buried my more embarrassing moments for fear of being judged as faulty. I refused to admit my thoughts and beliefs that often conflicted with the subculture of which I am a part. I chronically pretended that the darkest moments of all never even happened.

It wasn't just me I was protecting and running from, either. For some reason, I spent so much energy protecting those who often only hurt me. It was as if acknowledging that there were unhealthy people in my life, and admitting that their actions did actually affect me, would somehow reflect poorly on me and would make me even more transparently imperfect.

Finally living an authentic life freed me from all of that, and it let me be what every person in this world most certainly is, and it let me have what nearly every person in this world wants more than anything. It let me be flawed and it let me love and value myself anyway.

I have learned that the past doesn't actually exist. Not really. It is all just memories of what once happened, nothing more. What exists is our present selves. Our present minds and our present thoughts. The past *is* our present because it created every thought that we now have.

It is our pasts which create the lessons that will push every action of our futures.

This is why the stories of our lives are so important. Each story we carry is a fascinating slice of the past as we remember it, and with it will always come a greater lesson, big or small.

The ultimate question is, what lessons will we each learn? What will we take from it all? What emotions will we continue to let ourselves feel as we think back to those stories from our lives?

Will we feel resentment and anger at the people and events from our past? Will we look back with only fondness? Will we laugh whole-heartedly at the stupider things we did? Will we maybe even laugh at the hardest and most painful times?

How we remember the stories from our lives, and how we recount them, is what will make and break our entire existences. It is the stories of our past that will either keep us chained down into that repeating cycle of failure, or will free us to move forward and take our lives for ourselves.

Had I written this book five years earlier, the stories would have been very different. Many of them would have been pushed and driven by anger or resentment instead of by humor and introspection. They would have placed much more blame on others and much less of it on myself. It would not have been an enjoyable book for anyone to read, yet that book would have been filled with many of the same stories.

This is the biggest advantage we all have been given in this life. We *all* have the ability to see our stories and to tell those stories in new ways, and with renewed laughter, no matter how we have seen and told them before.

These are my stories. They are my life and my lessons learned. They are me, nothing more, nothing less. Take them or leave them, love me or don't. I really don't care. I'm going out for sushi.

Um…

That was the end.

Seriously. *Why* are you still flipping pages? This book *ended* like thirty pages and twenty minutes ago.

Wow, you awesome little rebel, you. Well, as long as you've clearly got nothing better to do, and you obviously are going to keep going with this, can I make a quick, shameless request?

And when I say shameless, I mean *shameless*...

Okay, here goes.

I self-published this book. If you somehow read it in its entirety (well, done, I didn't know if you'd make it), can I ask you for two favors?

First, leave an honest review in the online store from which you purchased it. And by honest, I mean 5-stars, with nothing but praise and accolades. Oh, wait. No. I *want* honest. 100% honest. Even if that means you hated the entire thing and you wish there was a ½ star option. I may cry because you have no soul, but I'll appreciate you taking the time to do it.

Second, if you enjoyed this book, please recommend it to... oh, I don't know... EVERYONE?! I depend on you, my dear readers, to please help me in this department. I have always been and will always be so appreciative.

Here is a small list of ways you should definitely, or definitely not, recommend it:

- Spray paint your recommendation onto a passing elephant's bum.
- Print millions of copies of your recommendation onto leaflets and drop them out of airplanes over big cities.
- Get arrested for doing something ridiculous and blame reading this book when the news cameras show up. There is no bad publicity, right?
- Promise on your social media walls that giant fortunes will show up in the mail the next day for anyone who gets a copy of this book. You can also claim that people don't love Jesus, or that they'll have bad luck for ten years if they don't. Hey, it works for other stupid internet crap.
- Or... just post it on your social media walls all classy-like or suggest it for your next book club read? Honestly, this may be the best and safest option. Yeah, go with this one.

ABOUT THE AUTHOR

I'm Dan Pearce, or as a friend once told me to shout from the rooftops any time life gets tough or I'm feeling particularly down about myself… "I'M DAN FUCKING PEARCE!"

And, shoot. After this book, I feel like you know way more about me than anyone probably should, so an "About the Author" paragraph is probably just overkill. Let's hang out and have fun on the internet together instead:

Read my blog or contact me at:
www.danoah.com

Join me on Facebook at:
www.facebook.com/singledadlaughing
www.facebook.com/mrdanpearce

Find me on Instagram:
@danoah

Bruce County Public Library
1243 Mackenzie Rd.
Port Elgin ON N0H 2C6

CPSIA information can be obtained at www.ICGtesting.com
Printed in the USA
LVOW10s1922250216

476707LV00031B/1269/P